# SECRETS FROM AN INVENTOR'S NOTEBOOK

## ADVICE ON INVENTING SUCCESS

## MAURICE KANBAR

### FOREWORD BY PHIL BAECHLER
### INVENTOR OF THE BABY JOGGER

Cover and interior design by
Blue Design, Portland, Maine
(www.bluedes.com)

Cover photographs of the author are copyrighted by Kevin Morris and Philadelphia University and used with their permission. All other images in the book are copyrighted by their respective rights-holders and used with their permission.

ISBN 978-1-5717-8328-8

Library of Congress Cataloging-In-Publication Data is on file with the Publisher.

Printed and Bound in the USA

First edition

10 9 8 7 6 5 4 3 2 1

Groups wishing to order this book at attractive quantity discounts may contact the publisher at info@counciloakbooks.com.

Council Oak Books, LLC
2822 Van Ness Avenue, San Francisco, CA 94109
www.counciloakbooks.com


Distributed in the United States and Canada by Publishers Group West.

# CONTENTS

# Foreword

I wish I'd had this book when I first invented the Baby Jogger®! It's a long road from a wild idea to a commercially successful product, but Maurice Kanbar has written a delightful map to help navigate that route successfully: from prototyping and market research, to patenting, manufacturing and selling a finished product.

The first step after that light bulb flashes on over your head is prototyping. For me, that consisted of welding some bicycle wheels onto an old rusty stroller I picked up for five bucks at a secondhand store. (Hey, don't laugh: some software billionaires started with IBM-PC computers.) In the chapter on prototypes, this would fall into the category of "functional prototypes." It was an ugly stroller, but it worked, and it was the first step in the evolution of the Baby Jogger®.

One of the biggest bumps on the road to success can be protecting your patent rights. When I started almost three decades ago with little more than a handmade stroller, one of the few information resources I could find was a skinny brochure from the U.S. Patent Office. Trust me, what you're holding in your hand goes way beyond that meager information source.

Filing and enforcing a strong patent can be a complicated process, but Maurice's book is chock full of real world experiences and examples, both from his and other inventors' case histories, told in a tone that's closer to an action-adventure movie than a dry how-to manual. The patent office plays by strict rules, however, so even such procedural details as how to document the inventive process are clearly explained (When I start a new stroller design, I keep all the documentation in a "Baby Book!") Most of us wouldn't do surgery on ourselves, so when it's time to find a good attorney, Maurice even has tips on selecting a firm to help you get the most bulletproof patent possible.

Of course, not all inventions are big winners. The old saying about "invent a better mousetrap and the world will beat a path to your door"—I can't remember the last time I bought a mousetrap. That's just the point! It's the NEW stuff that people are buying. I grew up listening to 45-rpm records. My kids don't even know what those are. The pace of innovation is increasing and there are always new gizmos coming on the market. You may have such a gizmo, or just an idea. Many times people have heard I was an inventor and confided in me: "Hey, I've got an idea." Some of those brainstorms actually were pretty good, but most of the time I never see the person again, or their product. Let's face it, getting to market can be tough. Sometimes it takes a lot of cash, and I typically warn people not to sell their house to start a business. (When I started my business I didn't even own a house to sell!) It's possible you have an idea that's good enough to patent and then license to an established company. That route could have some pitfalls, though, and there are plenty of sharks out there who would love to "help" you get your invention to market, namely their market. There are even firms, Maurice points out, that may lure you into a license deal just to keep your product from competing with theirs. Whether you want to find a manufacturer to do the work for you, or simply turn the product over to someone else on a royalty basis, Maurice's detailed analysis of the process could help you avoid nasty surprises and get the best deal.

The bottom line, as they say in business, is that the consumers vote with their dollars. Selling a product is one of the mainstays of American life. Turn on your TV and you'll see what I mean. We are bombarded by messages, and getting attention in a crowded marketplace is a major challenge. It was a long road from the time I started running in races with the Baby Jogger®, to the point at which it was showing up in movies or in tabloids being pushed by sunglass-wearing movie stars.

With SKYY® Vodka, Maurice faced the same marketing challenges. How could a little upstart vodka in San Francisco take on the established brands? It took a lot more than just a blue bottle, so the book's final segment on launching a successful brand reads like a fast-paced MBA in marketing that even non-inventors can enjoy. Can I mention Jack Nicholson and David Letterman? Just did.

I don't know how many folks have called me for advice over the years and I've spent hours talking about prototypes, patents and marketing. Now I can tell them to get this book, because it's all in here. I especially liked the references listed in the Appendix. Much of my patent and litigation experience has been by the school of hard knocks—this book provides a much easier, more effective and cheaper way to quickly get on the right track. Not only that, it's a lot more fun to read than patent abstracts or legal briefs. So, if you have an invention or even just a glimmer of an idea, get your thinking cap ready!

**- PHIL BAECHLER -**

# A Profile
## by Julian Guthrie

Maurice Kanbar takes a small X-Acto®
knife out of his jacket pocket and slices off the snags on the tablecloth at
Perry's on Union Street. Then he sets one of his inventions, called Zip
Notes™, on the table, pushing a button and tearing off a sticky note.

"This is the equivalent of 600 three-by-three Post-It® notes," he says of
the Zip Notes™ reel. "I was using Post-Its®, and they kept getting stuck
together, and sometimes you just want to write one thing and don't need
a 3-inch piece of paper. With this, you can have whatever size you want."
He adds, "Like most of the things in my life, this came about because I
thought, 'There has to be a better way to do it.'" Putting the X-Acto® knife
away, he laments that someone else thought of the cutting device first.

Kanbar, a compact and energetic octogenarian (he won't give his exact
age), is the inventor of things big and small, from SKYY® Vodka - with the
distinctive cobalt blue bottle - to SooFoo™, a nine-ingredient rice and lentil

mixture, from a D-Fuzz-It® comb for clothing to durable, collapsible and cheap eyeglasses for people in developing countries.

A San Francisco resident since 1984, Kanbar rides around town on his red scooter, gives a great deal of his fortune away, and admits he's something of a "cheap bastard," parking in spots where the meter is already paid.

Above all, though, Kanbar is a consummate tinkerer, a modern-day Buckminster Fuller, designing and inventing, theorizing and dreaming, sometimes kvetching and always in motion. Kanbar, with 35 patents over 40 years, admits with a sigh: "I put myself to sleep thinking about all of the problems I'm unable to solve."

## INVENTOR OF NECESSITY

Born and reared in Brooklyn, Kanbar turned to inventing out of necessity. His parents, Meir and Hannah Kanbar, didn't have much money - Meir operated a small laundry - and gave young Maurice and his two brothers, Elliott and Edward, one silver dollar at each birthday. Kanbar's first invention was a bow and arrow made out of branches, using cotton for the arrow's tip.

Harvey Roer, Kanbar's friend since the first grade, recalls the startup he and Kanbar launched when they were both around the age of 12. "We started a company together doing baby portraits," Roer said. "We made our own business cards, and had our own camera and a darkroom. We did OK." In more recent years - the early 1960s - the two started a business manufacturing and selling synthetic fiber for ladies' hosiery. "Maurice was the CEO, and I was CFO," Roer said. "We sold the company to our biggest competitor."

Roer, who lives in Newport Beach, said, "Maurice is one of the dearest friends I've ever had and ever will have. He's just a sweet lovable guy. And that mind of his doesn't stop."

## BREAKTHROUGH IDEA

Once Kanbar had earned his degree in engineering from Philadelphia University, his parents warned that he was on his own financially. "From that point on, I had to make it happen myself," Kanbar says. "Fortunately, I was blessed with a creative mind. I always liked chemistry. I always liked inventing." But turning an idea into an invention was another thing. As Kanbar notes, quoting Mark Twain, "The man with a new idea is a crank, until the idea succeeds."

Kanbar's breakthrough invention was the D-Fuzz-It®, the device that removes fuzz balls from fabric. "I was leaning against a wall, trying to look cool and meet girls, and when I pulled away from the wall, I noticed some pills from my sweater had clung to the concrete," Kanbar says. He forgot all about the girls and focused his attention on the wall.

"I studied the rough texture of the wall and thought, 'Could I replicate the wall's texture in a small gadget I could use at home?'" He got a patent, created a model, listened to his mom, friends and lenders at banks tell him he was nuts, skimped and saved, and ended up making everything from the device to the packaging. The D-Fuzz-It® cost him 14 cents apiece to make, and retailed at 98 cents each. It made $200,000 in the first year. He was 21.

"Before Maurice starts anything, he asks himself, 'Is there a need for this?'" said his brother Elliott Kanbar. "When he decides there's a need for it, he goes off and tinkers with it and comes up with a solution. He really hasn't changed a bit. As a child, he was always thinking of things to improve. He's gifted, and I would say he was born with that."

In 1984, sick of the summer heat in New York, Kanbar headed to foggy San Francisco. In 1998, he bought an eight-story building in Pacific Heights. A year later, he caused a stir when he evicted all of the tenants so he could be the building's sole occupant. "Being a landlord was terrible," he says. "I was treated like the janitor. The tenants all were wealthy, not exactly on welfare, and they all had months to leave. Now I won't rent." By 2001, Kanbar had developed and sold SKYY® Vodka to Campari for about $300 million.

## COFFEE ANTACID

As the waitress at Perry's serves coffee, Kanbar smiles and sets another invention on the table. "People say coffee upsets their stomach," he says. "So I have this, *Caffeo*™, which takes away the acid, in coffee, wine, juice.

It's a natural mineral alkaline. I read that something like 400 million cups of coffee are drunk every day. So I invented this."

From his corner table at Perry's, Kanbar keeps an eye on his scooter, delighting in the fact that he doesn't have to pay for parking. After lunch, Kanbar heads up the hill to his building on Jackson Street. He punches the button for the seventh floor, where he holds meetings (he lives on the top floor and keeps the rest of the space open for friends and family to visit.)

## NEW VODKA PROCESS

He sits down at a table in the living room, filled with his inventions old and new. The biggest of the new may be his latest vodka, Blue Angel, which he says is even purer than SKYY® - which was billed as the first non-hangover vodka.

"I thought I was done with vodka," he says. "But I found a way to age vodka in two weeks that used to take 10 years in a barrel. I figured out a filtration process that removes the congeners, which are the impurities created through distillation. The filtration process goes through four steps, but the formula is a secret." Blue Angel, he says, is "ultrapure and super smooth. I want to get every bartender in the city to know about it."

Not one to sit still for long, Kanbar pops out of his chair and darts to another room, returning with his latest pursuit - a device that will alert a spouse or partner when a loved one's heart has stopped. He mentions the Safetyglide™ hypodermic needle protector, to prevent accidental needle sticks, and shows off the eyeglasses he's been working on. To prove their durability, Kanbar steps on a pair of the plastic specs, folds them back out and puts them on. They cost 75 cents to produce, and he's already distributed thousands of pairs in India.

## FILMMAKING VENTURES

Kanbar also talks about his other venture in the film business. He has become a film producer. In 2006, he produced his first feature film, the animated "Hoodwinked!" followed by "Hoodwinked Too." A longtime supporter of the arts, Kanbar - who founded the Quad, the first multiplex movie house in New York - has donated more than $10 million to endow the Kanbar Institute of Undergraduate Film and Television at New York University. His parents, he says, were Sephardic Jews, and Kanbar identifies culturally as Jewish. "I take pride in my being Jewish," he said. "If you have more on your plate than you can eat, find someone who is hungry."

Smoothing his sweater vest, he muses, "I just want to get a lot of stuff done." Kanbar also looks to the day when he has more time to do things like read, travel and paint. A corner of his penthouse, a nook with dead-on views of the bay, is where Kanbar does his paintings in acrylic. He is single but dating - he has never married - and says that one of his few regrets is that he never had children. Not one to dwell for long, he changes the subject. "My brother tells me, 'Are you crazy? What are you working for?' He'll say, 'Why don't you hire someone just like you?' I say, 'He wouldn't work for me if he were just like me.'"

## WORKS IN PROGRESS

Then, getting out of his chair again, he says he's just started working on something that could be big. Returning with his latest invention ("You can't write about this," he instructs), he talks about the idea's virtues and its potential market. He talks about the materials he's tried and how he landed on this latest idea.

Studying his work in progress, he says, "Am I going to ever stop inventing? Only when I stop thinking." At this, he is reminded of one of his favorite films, "Limelight" by Charlie Chaplin. In the film, Chaplin tells the story of being a young boy and asking his father for a certain toy in the window.

"The great line in that," Kanbar says, his eyes twinkling, "happens when the dad in the movie points a finger to his own head and says, 'Son, this is the greatest toy ever invented.'"

**- JULIAN GUTHRIE -**

# Preface

I've been inventing and launching new products since my early twenties. People have sometimes characterized me as a born inventor, and I suppose I wouldn't disagree—because inventing solutions to problems, improving devices and systems, and then taking those solutions and improvements into the marketplace has never felt anything but natural to me. For better or worse, I'm hardwired that way. I'm grateful to have been able to turn my natural inclinations—constant curiosity about the world around me, a determination to learn how things work and then make them work better, and an interest in how and why we buy things—into a successful career.

As a Brooklyn-born teenager, I spent several summers working in a summer camp in upstate New York. One summer I was in charge of the dining room, which was staffed by campers. I revamped the way we worked and created new systems and schedules. As a result the room ran smoothly, with none of the screw-ups or temper tantrums of previous summers. At the end of the season, my boss called me into his office. I was expecting a pat on the back, but instead I learned that he attributed our efficiency not to my innovations but to the exceptional group of workers we had that summer. I was disappointed but I learned a valuable lesson: innovate not because you want your efforts noticed but because you will know you've done your best. (And if at all possible, be your own boss!)

About twenty-years ago, I moved from New York to California. I'd had enough success with my inventions to kick back a little and enjoy a relaxed pace of life in San Francisco. But instead of slowing down, I stumbled on another problem I wanted to solve. In the process I invented and launched my most successful enterprise yet: SKYY® Vodka.

Since my lesson in the summer camp dining room, I'd been content to do my work in the background, getting satisfaction from my successes and learning from my missteps without much outside attention. After SKYY®'s success, though, I began to find that people were interested in how I did what I do. Business and media people were curious about how someone could come out of nowhere and be so successful in the spirits business. They wanted to know how an inventor could launch a vodka. Home based tinkerers and inventors wanted to know if I could teach them how to develop and profit from their own innovations. Instead of routinely being asked, "Are you crazy?" (a question inventors soon get used to), I started being asked if I could help other people learn how to be similarly "crazy." And publishing types started asking me to write a book.

Some of those publishing types were from Council Oak Books. Before anyone cries foul, full disclosure: Several years ago I purchased Council Oak Books, a small, respected but struggling publishing house. As you'll see in the following chapters, I don't relish the day-to-day running of businesses, and though I'm an avid reader, I had no interest in being a book publisher. So I hired talented and experienced book people to maintain and improve Council Oak. Their long efforts to pry a book out of me about my inventing life were finally successful for two reasons.

First, they reminded me that all author royalties from the book would be given to charity. One of the joys of making money is being able to give it away to worthy people and causes. When you have more than you need and realize you can't take it with you, you start giving it away. Now, those same folks have managed to convince me to publish a revised and updated version of my original book. A number of things have changed in the intervening years, most especially patent law and technology. I hope this new edition will bring would-be inventors current with what's new, and what remains the same, when it comes to inventing and selling their inventions. I have also added a section that provides the reader with some room to take and make notes as they read the book and a section where they can "doodle" and conceptualize their inventions.

Something I read long ago in a biography of Andrew Carnegie has stayed with me: He gave much of his enormous wealth away before he died and he noted that it had been much easier to make his fortune than to spend it intelligently. I'm certainly no Carnegie, but over the years I have taken great satisfaction in providing financial help to young filmmakers through The Kanbar School of Film and Television at NYU, and in supporting worthy causes like cancer research through the Strang Center and the ecological efforts of the Wildlife Conservation Society. All the author proceeds from the sale of this book will be donated to charitable organizations and enterprises through the Kanbar Foundation.

> *The value of a dollar is social, as it is created by society.*
> **RALPH WALDO EMERSON**

Second, after agreeing to give a talk one evening at The Learning Annex, I was persuaded that hearing about my experiences might be useful and even inspirational to aspiring inventors and entrepreneurs. That class was packed with people of all kinds who listened intently and couldn't ask enough questions. There are a lot of curious, thinking people out there with great ideas, and they're keen to hear how others have made ideas pay. I know I didn't have a lot of mentoring or encouragement as I was coming up. Though I think I was born to invent and don't think anyone could have stopped me from persevering until I'd done it successfully, a little friendly advice wouldn't have hurt. And as I looked back over my business life, I saw that I hadn't been simply following my gut; I'd been following some rules, rules that anyone could learn.

Plus, I truly revel in the successes of other inventors, some of whom you'll meet in this book. When a Sam Farber (OXO Good Grips™ kitchen utensils), or Phil Baechler (the Baby Jogger®), or Ann Moore and Lucy Aukerman (the Snugli) parlays his or her hard work and ingenuity into a marketplace winner, I'm filled with admiration.

I hope reading about what has worked for me—and what hasn't—helps you. The basic how-to steps of inventing aren't mysterious. But executing each step and inventing a success can be confusing and difficult. If it weren't, every new product launched would be a hit. And most ventures, even in our current boom economy, are not.

I've written this book both to illustrate the concrete steps inventors take (from brainstorming and brand naming to prototyping and patenting) and to demystify the process so that you'll feel more confident about taking your first or next step. I look forward to reveling in your success.

**—MAURICE KANBAR, SAN FRANCISCO**

# Introduction
## THE D-FUZZ-IT STORY

The dude ranch was my friend Martin's idea. It was the mid-sixties and he'd heard this was a good place to meet women. So there we were, a couple of twenty something Brooklynites, doing our best rugged cowboy impersonations.

I was leaning against a wall, trying to look cool. I don't think my red sweater vest helped, but I always wore one. Martin was chatting up a couple of likely candidates and motioned for me to join him. When I pulled away from the wall, I noticed some pills from my sweater had clung to the concrete. "What are you looking at, Maury?" whispered Martin. "Get over here!" But it was hopeless. I couldn't stop thinking about how efficiently the wall had removed the annoying balls that form on sweaters. As usual, I couldn't rest until I figured out how the wall had restored my sweater. I was used to people like Martin getting impatient with the way my mind works. I'd been the kind of kid who not only asked why, but also how. It drove my parents nuts! My father would come home from a long day of work at the small laundry he owned and settle into his easy chair with the paper, only to have me ask how the lamp by his chair worked. He'd mumble something about electricity coming from the wall into the light bulb, but that didn't cut it for me. I needed to know how electricity worked.

I studied the rough texture of the wall instead of trying to charm our new friends. It must be the sharp edges of the sand crystals in the concrete that pulled off the fuzz, I thought. Could I replicate the wall's texture in a small gadget I could use at home? I thought such a tool would be a practical way to care for sweaters, much better than the brushes that were currently on the market. I knew I'd buy one, so I got to work.

Though I'd never invented anything, I knew that an invention is a thing, not just an idea. I'd studied engineering and chemistry in college, so when I got home I began experimenting. I bought some coarse fabric and sprinkled it with glue and aluminum oxide crystals (the stuff in sandpaper). I figured that it was a bit like concrete, with its rough surface, and might grab. I let it dry and then ran it over one of my sweaters. It worked beautifully. My crude but functional model was simply the abrasive-coated fabric stapled to a piece of wood.

I wanted to protect my invention with a patent and I had heard that you don't need a clean and shiny working model in order to apply for one. The Patent Office stopped requiring them when they ran out of storage space! My college roommate's cousin Herbie was a patent attorney, so I went to see him for help. He knew this was to be my first patent and wanted to make sure I wasn't too starry-eyed about the whole thing. "Look," he said, "I want you to understand that probably one in ten applications for a patent is granted. But out of those issued patents, I'd say that only one out of a hundred is ever manufactured. What's more, of those that are manufactured, maybe one in fifty is successful. You'd better be confident." I was. You've got to have guts to stick with your invention because many successful ventures were once considered ridiculous by lots of people. Despite Herbie's cautions, I applied for and was issued a patent.

My next step was to create a better model, something closer to the actual product I hoped to sell. I envisioned an inexpensive, durable plastic handle. A few blocks from my home there was a shop with a "Plastic Molding" sign in the window. I went in and talked to a model maker who said that sure, he could make a mold and prototype of my device—for $1,200. Unfortunately, I had used up my savings on another scheme that hadn't yet come to fruition. While working for a company that distributed DuPont fabrics, I had devised a unique method for manufacturing nylon fibers at a price competitive with that of DuPont. It would take several tries, though, before the pilot operation clicked, and I was eventually able to sell the enterprise to a Fortune 500 company, the largest women's hosiery manufacturer in the country. But that happy ending was a few years away and I needed the cash now for my plastic handle.

I tried to get the $1,200 for the mold at a few banks, but none of them would lend me money because I had no money to begin with. They only like to provide loans when they know you can pay them back! So I asked my mother for it. "Don't be crazy!" she said. "Why do you want to do that when you have such a nice job? Keep your job, honey."

But I didn't want to keep my nice job. I'd long known that I didn't want to be someone else's employee. So I saved the $1,200 by pinching pennies for eight months. I even told my dates they could only order a hamburger and a coke when I took them out because I was on a strict budget. I stuck with my strict budget because I had faith in my idea—and I'm stubborn.

When I'd saved the money, I had a one-cavity steel production mold made. A four-cavity mold would have made four times as many pieces in the same amount of time, but it would have required a greater initial financial outlay. We made our first samples with the one-cavity mold and invested in a four-cavity when the number of orders warranted it. (Each additional cavity in a mold significantly increases its cost. Even if one can afford more, it's prudent to do initial production runs with one-or-two cavity molds.)

Mold in hand, I started working on packaging. Because I was broke again, I couldn't afford to pay a graphic designer the $2,000 he wanted to design a hanging card to hold the device. While I didn't know a thing about packaging, I did know that cosmetic companies spent a lot of time and money perfecting theirs. So I went to drugstores and studied make-up boxes and bottles of shampoo. I bought products that featured typefaces and designs I liked and wrote some simple, descriptive copy: "Brushes away sweater fuzz in seconds . . ." I talked a friend who was between jobs into going in on the venture with me for a percentage of the business. The two of us scraped together $50 to pay another designer to do up our copy and design. And voilà, we had a professional looking product. I actually wanted to call my invention "Balls Off!" but this was 1964 and everyone said, "Are you crazy? [I get asked that a lot.] You can't call it Balls Off!" For once I relented and went with a name my friend Helen Shufro came up with: the D-Fuzz-It® Sweater and Fabric Comb.

The next problem—and it seemed like a big one— was how to get the D-Fuzz-It® into stores. We certainly couldn't afford to hire a sales rep. I went to a library reference room and found a list of department stores, with contact names and addresses. I wrote a short letter to the buyers in sweater departments. At the bottom of the letter, beneath a dotted line and the words, "cut here," I included a simple order form. I mailed off hundreds of these, along with sample D-Fuzz-Its®. Because the buyers could try the sample and see that it worked, I got orders. Hundreds of orders, then thousands.

Each D-Fuzz-It® cost us about 14¢ to make. We sold them for about 40¢ and they retailed for 98¢. We made $200,000 that first year, quite a lot of money at the time. About six years later, I let my partner buy my part of the business. All these years later, the D-Fuzz-It® sweater comb is still a reliable profit-maker. My package copy has even been translated into several languages because the comb is now sold internationally.

"I'm glad I was wrong," my mother told me at the time. By my thirtieth birthday, I never needed to work for anyone else again. No more dude ranches either. Not long after, I found myself on the David Susskind Show as one of the Five Most Eligible Bachelors in New York.

# The Five Steps To Inventing A Success
The Fundamental Things Apply

**M**any years, more than thirty patents, and several million dollars later, I still follow the same five fundamental steps I learned from inventing and marketing my first successful product, the D-Fuzz-It® sweater comb.

1. *Solve a Problem*

2. *Prove Your Invention/Build a Prototype*

3. *Protect Your Idea*

4. *Manufacture or License?*

5. *Market with a Twist*

From the humble D-Fuzz-It® to the high-end SKYY® Vodka, nothing has changed my approach—neither the technical Internet revolution nor the fact that banks now come knocking on my door. With experience, you get better at each of these steps, and you may sometimes be tempted to skip or scrimp on one or two. But there really are no shortcuts. Each step must be executed thoroughly and you must ruthlessly review your progress at every turn. Is this problem really worth solving? Do I have what it takes to solve it? Does my design meet each consumer requirement? Is this the perfect name? How can I make it even better?

Because these five steps are so important, the following chapters are organized around them. Each chapter begins with the story of one of my inventions, one that illustrates the task at hand. Then, because each step is made up of many others, we'll take a close look at the how, when and why of the real-world process. An appendix follows, filled with practical resources, suppliers, organizations, phone numbers, publications and websites. But let's start at the beginning, with a question inventors get asked all the time, "How did you get that idea?"

# 1.

# Solve a Problem

## You Oughta Be in Pictures: The Quad Cinema

At a Manhattan dinner party in 1972, I met a young man whose family owned a number of movie theaters. He complained about how lousy business was. "TV is ruining us," he said. "People just don't go to the movies the way they used to."

As a regular moviegoer, I was surprised to hear this. I grew up when kids flocked to the theaters every Saturday afternoon to see the next episode of serials like *Flash Gordon* and *Buck Rogers*. On Friday and Saturday nights, when our parents made an evening out of dinner and a movie, there were lines around the block. Everyone seemed to go to the movies back then—and I still went.

But more and more, television was keeping families at home. Why go out when you could watch comedy, drama, variety, sports and game shows while eating a TV dinner off of a TV tray? Watching TV was easy and free, unlike hiring a baby-sitter, finding a parking space and buying tickets, popcorn and soda.

The movie theater fellow said that his 1,200-seat theaters were lucky to have 120 people in them on most nights. I knew that it was true that television offered lots of entertainment, and it made sense that young families would find it easier and more economical to stay in, but by his own admission, some people were still going to the movies. Who were they?

I resolved to find out and did some "market research," attending movies and counting the house. I saw that the theater owner was right: no matter what the size of the theater, there were generally only about a hundred people at any given screening. And the people I saw were mainly in their twenties and thirties. I concluded that young people were still going to the movies on dates. Why were they still venturing out? If this was the core audience that could be counted on, it seemed important to understand their motivation.

Part of my inventor's approach is to think problems through by working out scenarios in my head and by talking to myself. If you try this, don't let your imagination run away with you. You must work with the things you actually see and hear around you in the real world and apply solid logic. This is remarkably good for understanding what people are actually thinking and what is motivating their actions. Here is what I concluded about the preponderance of young folks in the theater: Joe is interested in Mary and would like her to wind up at his place at the end of their evening. Joe could call Mary up and invite her over to see a movie on TV but she might think, "Not so fast, buddy" or "How cheap!" But if he calls her up and invites her out for dinner and a movie, he might just get her over to his place afterward. What better motivation could there be? There may have been a sexual revolution going on, but dating hadn't disappeared. And my common sense told me that there was also a percentage of the population that would always want the eventlike feel of going out to enjoy a film with other people. We crave the communal experience. Bottom line: Fewer people were interested in going to the movies regularly, but I concluded that there were some people who always would.

> *Always search for the cause of something unexpected.*
> **GUY KAWASAKI,** *RULES FOR REVOLUTIONARIES*

So, I reasoned to myself, TV had diminished the movie-going audience, and TV was here to stay, but there was still a smaller audience that could be relied upon. If you have a smaller audience, you obviously don't need a thousand-seat theater. How do you turn a profit when you are selling fewer tickets?

"What if you used the same space you'd use for a thousand-seat theater on several smaller theaters?" I asked myself. Rather than one movie bringing in a hundred people, you could have four movies each bringing in a hundred Joes and Marys. Instead of concentrating on increasing the number of customers for one film, why not increase the number of offerings? With only a relatively small increase in ticket takers, concession-stand workers and ushers, you could easily multiply your profit. And instead of complaining about your shrinking audience, you'd be giving that audience more viewing choices and a novel atmosphere.

I felt ready to build a model and test my idea. At the time, I owned two small buildings in Manhattan. I had a lab where I worked upstairs in one, but I couldn't rent the ground floors—hard to believe given today's crazy New York real estate market. I decided to turn the buildings into four small theaters.

I knew I needed a distinctive name, something modern that let people know this was a new kind of cinema. While the theaters were being built, I held a contest among my friends. "Come up with a catchy name," I said, "and I'll give you a year's pass to the movies." Soliciting ideas from a variety of people, of all ages and all walks of life, is a good naming technique. And contests are a tried-and-true method of involving potential customers in your process. The Planters Peanut Company got their Mr. Peanut graphic from a teenager who entered a contest they sponsored to create a trademark.

One friend suggested I call my theaters Movies 4. The name I liked best was the Quad Cinema. I gave the names my scenario test. When Joe called

Mary or (given the seventies' sexual revolution) when Mary called Joe, would they say, "What's playing at the Movies 4?" or "Let's go to the Quad?" The Quad rolled off the tongue more easily. It was simpler and catchier. So four months later, my two vacant buildings became Greenwich Village's Quad Cinema.

Because we were the East Coast's first multiplex, publicity was no problem. The *New York Times, Village Voice,* and *Variety* all called us. This was news. We also placed ads like the one shown above.

Just as with the D-Fuzz-It®, and because the movie exhibition business was in such a slump, plenty of people told me I was nuts to build the Quad. But we were profitable from the moment we opened in October 1972.

Because we were so successful, we soon had imitators. Businessmen like my dinner party companion saw our attendance figures in the trades and started cutting up their theaters.

What's happened to movie theaters since then hardly needs to be explained: many large old theaters were chopped up into several screens, and newly built multiplexes sprang up in suburban malls and cities across America, growing to ten, twenty screens, and more. Today, despite the fact that over sixty screens now show movies within a few miles of the Quad, it still turns a profit, showing the best independent and foreign films. The Quad is a New York City institution and, according to the recently deceased former Mayor Ed Koch, "one of New York's best off-beat film houses."

Unfortunately, many great old theaters have been demolished. In addition, the megaplexes often cram as many people as possible into theaters the size of screening rooms for maximum profit. Neither of these developments makes me happy. Then again, many beautiful old theaters were able to stay in business by revamping themselves. And even the multiplex owners have been catering to the full range of moviegoers by showing blockbusters in large main halls and screening edgier or foreign films in smaller theaters. The movie exhibition business survived by innovating, and it grew healthier and more exciting because of the greater number of screens. The end result for movie fans, like me, is more choice. I give that two enthusiastic thumbs up.

> *The man with a new idea is a crank—until the idea succeeds.*
>
> **MARK TWAIN**

As a postscript to the Quad story: some time ago, a friend pointed out to me that two other men claim to have invented the

. The late AMC Entertainment CEO Stan Durwood said he built the first two-plex in 1963 in Kansas City because structural issues in a building prevented the construction of one big theater. He followed up with a four-plex in 1966. Apparently, one James Edwards disputed this. He claimed to have invented the first multiplex (a two-plex) in Alhambra, California, in 1939. I have no interest in entering this who-did-it-first fray. What I know is that I hadn't heard about these theaters when I built the Quad, which was certainly the first multiplex in New York City, and by all accounts, the first multiplex on the East Coast. I'll take all credit—or blame—for that much.

## WHAT'S WRONG WITH THIS PICTURE?
## OBSERVATION AND CURIOSITY

As we've seen with the Quad Cinema and the D-Fuzz-It®, the inspiration for inventions can come from just about anywhere. When people ask me where I got the ideas for a four-plex and a sweater comb, I tell them: At a dinner party and a dude ranch. But the keys are observation and curiosity.

Inventions solve problems. You can't see problems if you aren't observant, and you won't invent solutions if you aren't curious. People sometimes think inventors sit in a chair and get marvelous ideas out of thin air, but that has not been my experience. Our inventor's DNA drives us to stick our noses into things and ask questions. If I hadn't observed what that concrete wall did to my sweater, I'd never have thought, "I think I'll invent a device to care for sweaters today." And if I hadn't been curious after a chance conversation about the movie exhibition business, I would never have come up with the four-plex concept. When your ideas are prompted by observations and curiosity about the world around you, you stand a better chance of inventing things that other people will care about and need.

The political, economic and humanitarian problems in the third world concern me for any number of reasons. How can the inventor's mindset help solve that? I heard that poor vision places a drag on the economies of developing nations. You can't work if you can't see. As one small step toward helping these people help themselves, how about some simple, nearly indestructible glasses that are cheap to produce and can be given away by the thousand? I developed some that consist of flexible polypropylene frames that hold perfectly round lenses. Lenses are delivered in bulk, in four diopters of plus-one through plus-four. There is also a test frame holding lenses in all four diopters. The patient looks through each lens in the test frame and says which works best for each eye. Maybe one eye needs plus-two and one needs plus-three. You snap the correct lenses into the frames on the spot and send the person on his or her way. There is no custom grinding or astigmatism correction, so perfect 20/20 vision is unlikely. But they'll get a life-changing improvement nonetheless—maybe they'll go from a natural 20/400 to a corrected 20/30. The design is basic but when you're trying to keep your hands out of the machinery or mend your clothes by the light of an oil lamp, aesthetics are not a top priority. They cost us 85 cents a pair to produce and we've given away over 55,000 so far in Nepal and other places. There is great satisfaction in putting your inventor's mindset to work on a wholly humanitarian project.

I once had an employee who marveled at my insatiable curiosity. One day he commented that he figured I could probably improve the light switch on the wall, if I considered it long enough. I think he's right—not because I'm such a brilliant fellow, but because I love to think about such things. I can't understand boredom because there's always something to look at and think about. More than that, I try to get behind things, to see how they really work and once I do that, I try to imagine how I can make them better. The how-does-that-work questions that used to drive my parents batty are the basis of inventive thinking.

*The important thing is to not stop questioning.*

**ALBERT EINSTEIN**

Back during my days with SKYY® I got intrigued with the chaotic ways an empty yogurt container bounced when it fell on the floor. Thus inspired I invented a simple bounce game that we used as a SKYY® promotion.

Recently, Anton Willis invented the Oru™ folding kayak[1]. There are other folding kayaks but his is radically different because it is based on the principles of origami and it folds really flat, really quickly. He had lived in highly rural Mendocino County, California, but had to get rid of his large fiberglass kayak when he moved to a small San Francisco apartment. The problem? Kayaks were too big. The inspiration? An ancient oriental art that makes something big out of something flat. The process? A lot of hard work and over twenty prototypes. The advantages? Easy portability, easy storability, quick assembly, and lightweight. Sounds like a winner.

When that theater owner began complaining to me about his family business, I could have nodded politely and then forgotten all about it. We were, after all, just making small talk and what did the movie theater business have to do with me anyway? But when I heard that theaters were empty, I was curious enough to wonder why. My informant didn't have a good answer, so I set myself to the task of finding out. I knew that problems are opportunities for inventors—if we can figure out how to solve them.

When you encounter a problem, begin by asking questions—the more basic and naive the better: Where does it happen? Who is affected by it and cares about it? How does it happen? When did it begin? Why is it important? (Gelb 1998, pp. 67-68)

I did some research. Movie attendance had peaked in 1946 when two-thirds of the American population went to the movies at least once a week. In the 1950s, with the arrival of black-and-white television, the movie business turned to color, 3D technology and Cinemascope to compete, but movie audiences steadily dwindled. By the 1960s, the movie-going population was only a quarter of its 1946 size. During the Golden Age of TV, a movie house manager put a sign on his theater door that read, "Closed Tuesday—I want to see Berle, too!" referring to Milton Berle's popular Texaco Star Theater. Clearly my theater-owning friend was right to rail against television. But I knew that TV wasn't going anywhere. As Federico Fellini is reported to have said, "To attack television would be as absurd as launching a campaign against the force of gravity" (Winship 1988, p. ix).

Just as talkies had lured audiences back into theaters during a mid-1920s slump in attendance, I reasoned that innovation could entice them back in the 1970s. I felt that the novelty and expanded viewing choices afforded by multiplexes were a way to hold onto and even expand the audience. As my Joe and Mary scenario showed me, and as my own movie-going experience confirmed, home entertainment could never replace the communal pleasures of seeing movies at a cinema, and there would always be a dependable ticket-buying population with reasons for going out rather than staying in. Movies and movie theaters are still big business even in these days of streaming video and Netflix, and the myriad of other entertainment opportunities offered by the Internet.

Another aspect of the theater business that could have discouraged me is the fact that distributors are reluctant to give smaller theaters their biggest pictures. Instead of treating this as a handicap, I made it our strength. With several smaller theaters, you can afford to show films that will attract a more limited audience. Almost from the beginning, the Quad made art, film festival and independent films its specialty. (We'll talk more about niche marketing later.)

The conclusions I made while coming up with the idea for the Quad were based on observation and common sense. In fact, the four-plex idea seemed so simple and obvious to me that I couldn't believe industry insiders hadn't thought of it themselves. But people who work in a particular field become used to doing business in set ways. They may say they believe in innovation, but in actuality they often cling stubbornly to "that's the way we've always done it" thinking. As an outsider, you have the advantage of viewing situations with fresh eyes and fewer preconceptions.

In *Rules for Revolutionaries*, former Apple Computer, Inc., chief evangelist Guy Kawasaki calls this outsider advantage "harnessing naiveté." He cites a great, possibly apocryphal, example from General Electric. In the 1930s, new engineers in the incandescent lighting group were welcomed with a practical joke. The initiation rite consisted of being assigned the "impossible" task of inventing "a coating for light bulbs that would remove the hotspot in the then current state-of-the-art design." No engineer was able to create this uniform glow bulb until around 1952 when a newbie did. He didn't know it was "impossible," so he wasn't trapped by a set of expectations (Kawasaki 1999, pp. 18-19).

Author Denise Shekerjian warns against "the twin opiates of habit and cliché... The more adept you are at something, the less likely you are to appreciate a varying interpretation... [or] generate new approaches." (Shekerjian 1990, p. 99). This was certainly true for movie theater owners in 1972. I didn't assume—like the veteran GE engineers—that since no one had come up with a solution there must not be one. And while theater owners thought the only solution to their problem lay in drawing more people, I saw the solution might be more movies. Don't assume you have to be an expert or an insider to invent and innovate.

> *Common sense is not so common and is the highest praise we give to a chain of logical conclusions.*
>
> **ELI GOLDRATT,** *THE GOAL*

If you are observant and curious, and if you get a kick out of thinking, you've probably imagined ways to improve existing products that you use every day. Bank employee George Eastman didn't invent the camera, but in 1877, after buying the bulky state-of-the-art model and all its accoutrements, he did recognize the need to make picture taking less complicated. He pioneered paperbacked film, doing away with heavy, breakable glass plates, and he kept innovating until, by the turn of the century, people around the world were taking pictures with his small, light Kodak box cameras (Newhouse 1988, p. 160).

Many of my inventions have been improvements on existing technology:

a more effective hypodermic safety needle, a mix of wholesome grains with a unique flavor, a more comfortable dental X-ray device, a better way to dispense sticky notes, a vodka less likely to give you a hangover, glasses cheap and durable enough to be given away. You know what they say about building a better mousetrap. Ask yourself the following questions about your improvement idea. If you can answer "yes" to even one of them, you may be on to something.

- *Is it more environmentally friendly or durable?*

- *Is it less costly or time consuming?*

- *Is it safer or easier to use?*

- *Is it smaller or quieter?*

- *Is it more comfortable or attractive?*

> *In the beginner's mind there are many possibilities, but in the expert's mind there are few.*
> **SHUNRYU SUZUKI,** *ZEN MIND, BEGINNER'S MIND*

And consider these ten techniques for fostering your creativity and enhancing your inventing life:

1. *Observe the world around you and be curious about what you see.*

2. *Study problems—think about why they exist, who they affect, and how they might be solved.*

3. *Ask questions of yourself and others.*

4. *Look up words you don't understand and subjects that are unfamiliar to you.*

5. *Recognize and embrace the advantages of being a nonexpert.*

6. Read as much as you can. (See the Inventor's Reading List on p. 47.)

7. Pay attention to surprises (fuzz balls on a concrete wall) and accidents (the bounce of a yogurt container), and make connections—think of ways to use that grabbing or bouncing (D-Fuzz-It®, SKYY® Bounce Game).

8. Carry a notebook to record your questions, insights and reflections.

9. Talk with others. Seek out intelligent give-and-take in a small group, with egos checked at the door, and with mutual criticism that requires each person to defend his or her positions.

10. Go to places like San Francisco's Exploratorium museum of science, art and human perception or Chicago's Museum of Science and Industry— places where the imagination and ingenuity of others are on display and may spark your own.

> Put an ingenious person in intimate contact with a problem and he or she will invent a solution.
>
> **ANNE L. MACDONALD,** *FEMININE INGENUITY*

## PROBLEMS: YOURS, MINE AND OURS

Observation and curiosity can lead you to unexpected and unforeseen places, including previously unfamiliar industries. But sometimes you need look no further than your own life. I wore sweaters all the time and I knew there was a need for a simple, inexpensive way to care for them; I wondered why alcoholic beverages gave me headaches and so I created a less-irritating vodka; I found myself annoyed at the typical pad of sticky notes so I invented a machine for dispensing them in any length needed.

The Baby Jogger® idea came to a runner who wanted to be able to take his infant son along on his runs. He knew that if the device he created in his garage solved his problem, it might also be of use to others. Teva sport sandals were developed by a Colorado River guide to solve the problem of wet athletic shoes for river rafters. The sandals then went on to become practical and popular for all kinds of outdoor activities (Thomas 1995, pp. 12, 174-75). Ann Moore and her mother, Lucy Aukerman, invented the Snugli soft infant carrier to satisfy Ann's desire to maintain nurturing closeness with her infant daughter while moving about (Macdonald 1992, p. 337).

One of my favorite problem-solving invention stories is that of the OXO Good Grips™ product line. Sam Farber, the founder of Copco, a successful cookware company, and his architect wife Betsey, were doing a lot of cooking together for their friends the summer Sam retired. They came to realize that none of the kitchen tools they were using met their needs. Betsey's mild arthritis made her especially aware that a hand tool is only useful if the tool-to-hand connection works well; Sam reasoned that there must be many people like them who, for one reason or another, and at one time or another, found handling kitchen utensils troublesome.

He telephoned Davin Stowell, founder of the industrial design firm Smart Design. Smart Design had previously done projects for Sam at Copco. Sam told him he wanted to develop a line of kitchen tools that would be comfortable, affordable, beautiful and dishwasher safe.

They tossed out the usual preconceived notions and started from scratch. Through consultations with experts and a long trial-and-error process of model making and testing (which we'll examine in greater detail in Chapter 2), they crafted a small line of kitchen tools based on the principle of Universal Design—products designed to be comfortable and easy to use for people of all ages and abilities. Farber came out of retirement to start up OXO and make Good Grips™.

The distinctive swivel peeler quickly became a favorite best seller and OXO's signature product. Today there are more than 850 products in the OXO and Good Grips™ line, and many were inspired by observed problems. Davin Stowell's messy experience of teaching his young daughter to bake cookies led to mixing bowls with nonslip bottoms.

Good Grips™ problem solvers have been honored with numerous awards, including the American Culinary Award of Excellence, the Good Housekeeping Good Buy Award, and a Tylenol®/Arthritis Foundation

Design Award. Their products have even been included in the permanent collection of the Museum of Modern Art in New York.

If your eyes and ears are open, as Sam Farber's were that day in his kitchen, you will notice how you or someone near you is compensating, making do, or fashioning a jerry-rigged solution to get something they need or want. Over the years, my interest in medicine and my conversations with a number of physician friends about the shortcomings of various medical devices have led me to create and license a number of medical instruments.

Remember: Problems are opportunities. Observe your own life and how others make their way through theirs. Let yourself be curious about the problems you see, and try to imagine how things might be better. Then arm yourself with the practical tools to make that potential solution a reality.

## THE REAL WORLD: MOVE FROM IDEA TO INVENTION

If I had to choose another career, I would teach introductory physics to non-science students. I think I'd make a good teacher, and I'm sure I could get kids excited about the little miracles we take for granted—texting or "Skyping" with people around the world, driving a car, switching on a light. Once kids understand the scientific principles behind these everyday acts, they see the world differently. Plus, when you understand how things work, you can start to think about improving them. I wish I'd had more adults around me when I was a kid who could answer my how-does-it-work questions, and I'd love to be able to excite kids about that kind of learning.

> *The desire to know is natural to good men.*
> **LEONARDO DA VINCI**

When I was growing up, one of the few adults to take my constant how and why questions seriously was the pharmacist I worked for as a teenager. I wasn't burly enough for the typical after-school job that most neighborhood kids did—boxing and delivering groceries at the A&P—so when I was twelve or thirteen, I started working for Saul, delivering prescriptions and helping out in the pharmacy.

One day I asked Saul how gold plating was done. He gave me a vague, preoccupied, adult kind of answer, but when I pressed him, he admitted he really didn't know. "Go to the library," he said. "Check out a book on electroplating and bring it to me. We'll read the book together and figure it out."

These days when I have that kind of question, I'm likely to call Al Kolvites, the head of my product development lab. Al is an engineer, a commercial pilot and an experienced product designer and developer. I graduated from the Philadelphia College of Science and Technology. But nobody knows everything! If I ask myself a question that I can't answer, such as, "How the hell do they brassplate objects? Brass is an alloy, how is it done?" I'll call Al and ask him. He'll say, "That's a damned good question," and set about answering it. Neither one of us may need to know the answer, but someday, in the process of fleshing out an idea, knowing how to brass plate something might come in handy. If noticing and being interested in a problem is the first step on the way to an invention, being capable of solving it is the second. So we make it our business to cultivate a broad base of knowledge. An understanding of materials and mechanisms is essential when you are trying to turn your idea into an invention. Invention favors the prepared mind.

In the early stages of your product development, after you've pinpointed a problem and while you are brainstorming solutions, but before you know exactly what your final product will be made of, you might use a stand-in substance. Al calls it "nonexisteum." Nonexisteum is infinitely light, infinitely strong and costs nothing. With it, you are free to be very creative and your plans proceed beautifully. But at some point, you have to get real and find an existing substance that will meet your design's demands. What kind of adhesive will withstand high temperatures? Which materials resist rust? What kind of fastener will keep manufacturing costs down? What will make this game safe for children? That's when it helps to know how things are made and how they work—and maybe even how to brass plate something.

The Wright brothers studied the principles of lift, thrust and control and they conducted lots of tests. They had this crazy idea for carrying a person through the air, but they slowly learned from all their testing and this enabled them to make their idea real. We wouldn't know whom the Wright brothers were if all they'd done was say, "We have an idea for a machine that flies through the air. You can ride in it and look down from it and it'll be great."

> *A man should keep his little brain attic stocked with all the furniture that he is likely to use.*
>
> **SIR ARTHUR CONAN DOYLE**

## IDEA VS. INVENTION

This brings up a very important point. With very rare exceptions, you can get a patent on an invention, but not on an idea.

What's the difference? According to the United States Patent and Trademark Office (USPTO), an invention is an idea that has been "reduced to practice." That means it's been turned into a real-world working object or device. Here's how that works.

Joe and Mary—our two moviegoers from earlier in the chapter—are driving back from the show. Compounding Joe's anxiety over whether Mary will ask him upstairs is the fact that it's drizzling. Joe is driving and keeps having to turn the windshield wipers on and off, on and off. He gets frustrated and says, "I wish there were some way to make these darned wipers run intermittently." Mary, who is actually a mechanical engineering student, thinks to herself, "I could do that by putting a cam on the wiper motor output shaft so it acts upon the dual wiper linkage, thereby…" and in her head she proceeds to design the whole thing. Meanwhile, Joe is really pleased with himself over his idea and is convinced he'll make a million dollars on it. Well, Mary is too distracted by visions of cams and linkages to notice that Joe would like to come upstairs so she says good night and dashes inside to draw up the whole thing. Joe is disappointed, but not for long. I'm happy to report that within a couple months the two are engaged. Meanwhile, Joe keeps dreaming about his wipers. But Mary has actually designed them, built a prototype in the garage, and filed a patent application for a "cam-driven intermittent windshield wiper device." Joe is unaware of this. Wedding bells ring. A patent is granted. She approaches the automakers, one of which gives her a small lump payment and an agreement to pay her a couple dollars on each cam-driven intermittent wiper unit they install. Joe finds out and is less than pleased. It's not a community property state and he wants the money and credit from "his" invention. After all, he came up with it first, didn't he?

Who invented this intermittent windshield wiper? Joe or Mary?

Legally, Mary did. Joe simply had an idea and smiled about it a lot. Mary actually took an idea and *reduced it to practice*. She made it real. The USPTO justifiably awarded her the patent and would have told Joe to take a hike. Whether Joe gets any of Mary's profits or not is up to the divorce lawyers.

So if you want to actually profit from your ideas, you have to make them work in the real world. With few exceptions, inventions are things, not ideas—though the U.S. Patent Office is issuing more and more patents for thoughts, processes and ideas in cyberspace. We'll look at patents in far more detail in Chapter 3.

Joe may have been a good idea person, but Mary exhibited the ability and passion to actually make something of it. Guy Kawasaki cites ability and passion as the most important traits of revolutionary innovators, like those who developed the Macintosh. He calls them "evangineers." They're evangelists who want to change the world, and they're engineers who have the technical knowledge to do it. (Kawasaki 1999, p. 30)

Acquiring this knowledge isn't that difficult. When making my first crude D-Fuzz-It® prototype, my science background told me that aluminum oxide might replicate that concrete wall's grabbing properties. But when I started to think about the Quad, I had to educate myself about the movie exhibition business. I observed the crowds in theaters, studied the industry's trade journals and talked to people about what was important to them in a theater.

It's been my experience that people like to talk about their areas of expertise. If you've done your homework, ask intelligent questions and are honest about your motivations, most people, especially experts, welcome your desire to understand their field. There's no need to disclose your potential invention. You aren't asking these people to invent for you, you are simply asking technical questions about materials or processes you might use. If the Wright brothers had asked a cabinetmaker, "What's the best way to laminate and glue wood so that it is light and strong?" is the cabinetmaker inventing the airplane? Of course not, so don't be shy— question authorities.

To keep our knowledge current, Al and I read widely in a variety of technical fields. Read what interests you. Read to answer a question that pops into your mind. Read when a problem arises and you don't know how to solve it. Read until your vision blurs because when you invent, you are almost always building on and using previously discovered information. Al and I subscribe to trade journals and industry publications, many of which can be accessed for free at libraries or on the Internet. We keep up with what's going on with things like lasers, plastics, adhesives and new prototyping tools like 3D modeling because we know that perfecting our next invention may require this kind of information. You should do the same.

Years ago, Al and a friend created a dimensional board game that they pitched to a major toy company. The game was called "The Spider and the Flies." A "web" sloped down to the spider's lair. Hidden magnets along the paths the flies took in their attempt to steal the spider's treasure randomly caused some flies to flip over and "die" before reaching their goal. Their vice-president of new products loved the game but ultimately passed on it. His research told him that the game would be too expensive to produce because of the intricate shapes and paths on the board. Today, with a great deal more knowledge about materials and the manufacturing process, Al could probably tell the toy company how to produce it economically. Knowledge like that can turn a red light green.

## INVENTOR'S READING LIST

1. *The Internet, for company home pages, patent information, product names, articles about everything you can imagine, and general research. Use the Internet to get ideas, but beware: there are millions of self-styled experts out there. You rely on their views at your peril; so once you have a couple of ideas, check them through reliable sources.*

2. *Your local and a national daily newspaper such as the* Wall Street Journal *or the* New York Times.

3. *Magazines such as* Forbes, Fortune, *and* U.S. News and World Report.

4. *A wide variety of product catalogs (and you thought that was junk mail!).*

5. *Trade journals and trade association publications.*

6. *Government studies, available from the U.S. Government Printing Office (www.gpo.gov), such as* Survey of Current Business, Business America: The Magazine of International Trade, Official Gazette of United States Patent & Trademark Office *of Commissioner of Patents and Trademark and the Economic Report of the President (see the appendix for addresses)*

When you have a broad base of knowledge you are better able to make connections. The ability to make connections is a key component of creativity that can also be vital to inventing solutions. When Al worked at InterMetro Industries Corporation, he was assigned to a shelving project. His task was to offer the customer shelving made out of something other than stainless steel, which is a great material because it doesn't rust, but which is also very expensive. His team came up with an innovative composite plastic shelf, based on existing technology pioneered, in part, by the aircraft industry. They reasoned that if this composite construction was strong enough for an aircraft wing, it was strong enough for a shelf. Al was able to make this connection because of his interest in aviation and aviation technology. The resulting shelving won awards for innovation and made

InterMetro a great deal of money. *Make connections.*

The OXO Good Grips™ Salad Spinner is the result of a trip to a toy store. The designers replaced the awkward cranks, winding mechanisms, and pull strings on existing spinners with a simple pump inspired by a child's spinning top. Again, a connection was made.

> *Therefore, the mechanic should sit down among levers, screws, wedges, wheels, etc. like a poet among the letters of the alphabet, considering them as the exhibition of his thoughts; in which a new arrangement transmits a new idea to the world.*
>
> **ROBERT FULTON**

How could being a film buff lead me to get a patent called "The Use of LEDs, Flashing at High Speed, to Reduce the Consumption of Electricity in Stoplights"? Because I'm interested in film and have had a lifelong fascination with vision, I knew that our eyes retain images on the retina for one-sixteenth of a second after seeing them. Motion pictures evolved from this understanding, set forth by Peter Mark Roget (the thesaurus fellow) in his 1824 paper, "The Persistence of Vision with Regard to Moving Objects" (Newhouse 1988, p. 171).

This fact led me to imagine the advantage of using a cluster of LEDs (light emitting diodes) in a stoplight. By flashing very rapidly they give the illusion of being on constantly, but they use substantially less power than a bulb that is on nonstop. I donated this patent to a university in hopes that they would be able to prove its value and safety, and thus get municipalities to use and benefit from it.

Another example: Some years ago I was discussing cataracts with an ophthalmologist friend when he told me about a cryogenic cataract-removal procedure he regularly performed on patients. Liquid nitrogen was used to freeze an implement that was then used to clear away lens fragments in the eye. I thought this sounded very dangerous—if there's a spill, liquid nitrogen can cause severe damage. I thought there had to be a better way and told my friend I'd think about it.

Elementary physics—what I turned to when my parents couldn't tell me how we got ice cubes in July—teaches us how a refrigerator works. Very basically, a liquid changing to a gas (evaporating) absorbs heat, making things colder. If you fill a chamber with a compressed gas then open that chamber and release the gas into a larger chamber, the gas will absorb heat.

My solution at the time was simple, though I wouldn't use the same materials today. Back then we weren't aware of or concerned about the ozone-damaging properties of compressed gas refrigerants, and so I filled a tube with Freon. A button push punctured the tube and the evaporating compressed gas made the tip of the instrument very cold. You could then touch the lens of the eye with this tip, freezing it and removing it intact.

My friend tried the model I made and thought it was fantastic. I sold the device to Alcon Laboratories, a company that specializes in ophthalmologic pharmaceuticals. They called it Cryophake and did very well with it. I could invent this device because I made the connections between elementary refrigeration physics and the need for extreme cold in a medical procedure.

Phil Baechler built a working prototype of his Baby Jogger® out of a used stroller and an assortment of bicycle and other parts. When Baechler and his six-month-old son unveiled the creation at a 10K race, some racers looked at them with bewilderment, and others with envy. Baechler was asked where he'd bought the device, and he realized he could have begun selling them right there and then—if he'd had more than one. He first needed to figure out how to create a manufacturable product.

Baechler experimented with framing tubes from pieces obtained at an aircraft plant and with both steel and aluminum tubing. All presented problems. A visit to a boating supply store with a friend proved serendipitous. There, Baechler found a plastic hardware connector used for boat railings that formed a strong yet flexible joint perfect for connecting aluminum tubing. Inspired by this, Baechler began designing his own connecting pieces using custom plastic molds, which eventually led to the first Baby Jogger® patent and a product that was innovative, well built, and more easily reproduced. Learning about materials and making connections are crucial (Thomas 1995, pp. 175-76).

## REALITY CHECK: REINVENTING THE WHEEL AND OTHER COMMON MISTAKES

Another aspect of getting real, one that comes up throughout the invention development process, is being realistic about whether you've found a problem that is worth solving, and/or whether your method of solving the problem is actually better than a solution that already exists. My Eleventh Commandment, one that reflects the unfortunate Achilles' heel of many inventors, is Thou Shalt Not Bullshit Thyself. Don't proceed past the idea and preliminary research phase until you are certain you have a viable invention.

As I've said, if your ideas are based on observation and curiosity about the world around you, the chances are good that the problems you tackle will be of interest to other people. But even when you set about solving a problem you've noted, it's possible to lose sight of the bottom line. To emphasize this common inventor pitfall, I offer the cautionary tale of 80/20 Cola. Never heard of 80/20 Cola you say? I'm not surprised, and I invented it.

Some time ago I was at a hamburger joint. I went to fill my soda cup but could not decide which to get—regular, with its good flavor and many calories, or diet with its unpleasant metallic aftertaste but very few calories? I tried an experiment, mixing about 20% regular and 80% diet. It tasted great. The sugar masked the artificial sweetener, but the whole thing had only a fraction of the calories of the full-sugar soda. I soon decided there was a potential product here, because you could get all the flavor with minimal calorie count.

Was I intimidated by the presence of Coca-Cola and Pepsi? I was not. I had just launched SKYY®, and RC Cola had been profitable for years with only about 1% of the cola market. I hired people and got a flavor laboratory to create a cola that tasted right with my 80/20 sweetener mix. We held the calorie count to 30 per can, one-fifth that of

regular soda. I even made sure it had 100% of the daily allowance of vitamin C, just for good measure. I oversaw the can design and hired distributors. I was sure America would just love our best-of-both-worlds solution.

It didn't.

We released it in June 2000 in Houston, without a lot of fanfare. Now there is no denying that the stuff is good. Everyone agrees on that. But America's cola attitude apparently is "Give me sugary or give me diet!" For whatever reason, the folks in the U.S.A. don't like a cola compromise. Both Coke and Pepsi discovered this at various times over the years when their own reduced-sugar options fell flat. Second, we realized too late that the profit margin on a case of soda was about eleven cents, which makes it extremely difficult for a small producer to succeed. Coke and Pepsi make it up on volume. A third factor was that my recipe, though protected as a trade secret, was probably not patentable. Even if it had been patentable, Coke or Pepsi could have taken the key element—the 80% aspartame and 20% sugar mix—and changed it slightly to 79%/21% to make their own version, backed by their huge distribution network and immense marketing budget.

What had happened? I sheepishly admit that I had broken my 11th Commandment, and had bullshitted myself. I had thought "Hey, they do it, why can't I?" when about ten minutes of research would have revealed the unworkably low margin. And I thought that just because I appreciated the value proposition (all the flavor, a fraction of the calories) everyone else would. I had created a solution when there was no problem.

Some would shake their heads and point out that I did no formal market testing or focus groups. Well such research would have falsely told me that I had a winner, because everyone who tastes this stuff loves it. In the real world, market testing and focus groups fail all the time. Focus groups are infamous for false positives, because people like to be agreeable. I'll bet Coke and Pepsi did plenty of research on their low-sugar versions but those products failed too. 80/20 Cola failed because of a market quirk and a miniscule margin, which formal market research would not have revealed. And the giants would probably have pushed me out eventually anyway. After a few successes it is easy to get cocky and to bullshit yourself.

In a story I like to call the Cottage Cheese Incident, I once spent a few hours looking into making my own cottage cheese, since the regular kind at the store wasn't much good and the really tasty organic stuff was $6.00 a quart. But in the end it wasn't worth the time spent sitting on a tuffet waiting for my own curds & whey to age.

Then there's the story of Iridium, the world's first handheld global satellite telephone and paging service. When I first heard about them, the company was facing bankruptcy and looking for a buyer. They had launched a network of sixty-six satellites to facilitate uninterrupted communication around the world. But as U.S. News Online reported (8/30/99), their phones were "too bulky and too expensive" and often didn't work well. Setting up had cost them over $5 billion, but they only attracted a few thousand users. They were eventually bought for $25 million[3] and currently operate as Iridium Communications, Inc.

I wasted more money on 80/20 Cola than I care to admit. I wasted a few dollars and a few hours on my perfect cottage cheese. The original Iridium wasted billions. The more you have to lose, the more careful—in fact, the more ruthless—you need to be in reviewing your plans. Ruthless reviewing should precede and follow each of your actions. Remember that Eleventh Commandment: Thou Shalt Not Bullshit Thyself. Always ask yourself the following:

- *Is manufacturing my idea feasible? Do I have some nuts-and-bolts ideas about how to carry it out?*

- *Is my idea worth implementing? Will it offer unique benefits over other products?*

- *Is it a clear winner? Is the market big enough to create decent profit margins in the not-too-distant future?*

It may help to be honest with yourself about these if you actually write out the answers in a business plan. Trying to formulate accurate and honest answers is a reality check, and it's easy to imagine trying to convince a potential investor. Believe me, investors are far less susceptible to bullshit than you are.

We'll talk more about this kind of project evaluation a little later, and I certainly don't mean to throw cold water on your enthusiasm. I agree with essayist Sydney Smith who wrote, "A great deal of talent is lost in this world for the want of a little courage." Goodness knows that I grab hold of my ideas like a pit bull and can't be dissuaded from pursuing the ones I believe in. If I had given up every time someone said, "Are you crazy?", I never would have developed some of my most successful inventions. But while you have to be passionate to bring an invention to fruition, you have to be dispassionate in assessing your ideas—before you spend a lot of time and money on prototypes and patents. Since the 80/20 fiasco I have rejected other product ideas on margin alone. What's the point, if you're not going to make a buck or have a buck to donate to someone else?

Think about marketing from the outset. Can you sell this beloved brainchild of yours? Remember, having a patentable invention is not the same thing as having a marketable one.

If you are confident that you've solved a problem worth solving, and that you've solved it economically and with clear value to potential consumers, pat yourself on the back. Now we'll get cracking on your prototype.

## (ENDNOTES)

1    http://www.orukayak.com/

2    *A Treatise on the Improvement of Canal Navigation* (1796), preface, x, http://todayinsci.com/F/Fulton_
     Robert/FultonRobert-Quotations.htm

3    Journal of Information Technology Management, A Publication of the Association of Management
     "GOOD TECHNOLOGY, BAD MANAGEMENT: A CASE STUDY OF THE SATELLITE
     PHONE INDUSTRY", by JAEJOO LIM, RICHARD KLEIN and JASON THATCHER, Journal
     of Information Technology Management Volume XVI, Number 2, 2005, http://jitm.ubalt.edu/XVI-2/
     article5.pdf

# 2.

# Prove Your Invention / Build a Prototype

This is the story of how a simple ingredient substitution led to a new and successful product line. My cousin and his wife Frida were in town for a few days, and for dinner one evening she cooked me a dish that I had never seen or heard of before. She said it was a very popular dish from the Middle East. I said, "Hey this stuff is great! What's in it?" She told me it was based on lentils and white rice. I put my fork down and said thanks anyway but I'll pass.

"What's wrong with it?" she asked.

"It's got white rice in it," I said.

"What's wrong with white rice?"

"White rice is 100% sugar," I said. "They make white rice by stripping off the nutritious bran and germ and feeding it to the pigs. You're left eating the starchy inner kernel and that turns completely to sugar in your system. The pigs eat well but you get diabetes."

She was kind of miffed. "It's good," I said. "The only problem is the white rice. Give me the recipe."

The next night I cooked her the same thing with organic brown rice and lentils. I like to cook and have a strong interest in healthy food. She said, "Hey this stuff is great! I think it's better with brown rice!"

So I had a delicious new recipe. But in my typical fashion I was not completely happy with it and kept wondering how I could make it better. I started experimenting, which by this time should come as no surprise to you. The first thing I did was to throw in some whole-wheat berries. This worked very well and added a nice mild crunch. I went to the local organic food store and bought a pound or so of a bunch of different bulk grains and such. I cooked up each one according to the recommended method, just to get used to how it's supposed to come out. One was too mushy, one was too hard, and one required too much boiling. Beans were inconvenient because they should really be soaked overnight. Others were great. I started combining things that I liked and that had similar cooking times. Some made pleasant combinations and some did not. I kept experimenting (with friends as reasonably willing test subjects), and we ate well on the results. In the end I had a combination of three different types of lentils, oats, barley, buckwheat, rye, long-grain brown rice, and those delicious wheat berries. It cooked up just like rice, and was really good even plain with a little salt. When I cooked it up with broth, vegetables and herbs it was better. When I put it in a stew with lamb or beef it was great. It became a staple on my table when I entertained friends.

One of these friends alerted me to the obvious: that I had a very promising product. It's high in fiber, has no fat, is vegetarian, vegan, and kosher. It's all organic. It provides a lot of value to the health conscious shopper. It's also very flexible, is easy to cook, and can be prepared in a number of ways and added to any number of dishes.

The first big thing to do was to find a name. Your product name should be unique, easy to pronounce, easy to spell, and it should make a good website address. You should test it in conversation to make sure it rolls off the tongue nicely. I tried combining the ingredient names in various ways but got nowhere with that. I thought of Grain-O but it sounded archaic (and I later found out that there was a coffee substitute in the late 19th century called "Grain-O"). I did not want anything silly like "Dr. Kanbar's Miracle Grains." When I described it to people I always found myself saying, "It's super good food!" That stuck with me but it was too long, too descriptive and too generic. I may not have been able to trademark it. After working with that a bit I shortened Super Good Food to SooFoo™ and that's what stuck.

I was also thinking about how to promote it. My first thought was to sell through retail grocery stores. I would have to package it appropriately and that would be no problem. We designed a colorful package that would appeal to consumers who want organic products.

I also wanted to offer it to vegan restaurants because they have a lot of limitations on what they can sell and are constantly looking for delicious new dishes. SooFoo™ is high in protein and that's always an attraction to vegetarians and vegans. Once a product catches on with a niche market, proprietors in other markets will often get wind of it and want to sell it as well. We made plans to offer a 25-pound bulk bag.

So with my basic plan in place I set about finding a way to obtain the finished bulk grains. I envisioned SooFoo™ from the start as an all-organic product. So I had to either build relationships with organic farmers or find someone who knew where to go for the right lentils, wheat, rice, and other ingredients. I decided on the second approach, and eventually hooked up with a compounder who now obtains all the certified organic grains and lentils I require. This compounder mixes them in the right proportions and packages it.

Now we had to see if we could actually sell it.

We approached the buyer for the Draeger's Market grocery store chain here in the San Francisco Bay Area. I brought a small Thermos-style bowl of cooked SooFoo™ with me. The buyer and others on the staff liked it and since it was in packages all set to sell he readily agreed to let us do a tasting. On the appointed day we set up our table and a SooFoo™ cooker (a small rice cooker emblazoned with the SooFoo™ logo). We offered it to folks as they passed by, and they loved it. We sold fifty-two packages, when usually it's considered a great success if a tasting sells just twelve to eighteen. Draeger's agreed to carry SooFoo™. We approached Whole Foods the same way we approached Draeger's and had virtually identical success.

We had pretty much proven that our target market liked it and that they would buy it. Now it was up to the marketing folks to spread the word further, get other chains to carry it, and to get it into restaurants, both vegan and otherwise.

We also discovered that it sells best in stores where we have conducted tastings, and that supports my desire to get it into restaurants so people can actually taste it. Restaurants (particularly vegetarian and vegan restaurants) are always eager for new and unique dishes to attract more customers. Once these customers discover how good SooFoo™ is in salads, soups, stews and sides, they'll look for it in their local grocery stores.

## OUCH! THE KANBAR TARGET

The Kanbar Target provided an entirely different kind of product and prototyping cycle. During a dentist appointment many years ago I needed X-rays. The technician put a heavy and painful contraption in my mouth to hold the film and told me to bite down and stay still. I tried to cooperate but it was so painful that I left without getting the pictures taken.

Annoyed and yet intrigued, I enlisted Al Kolvites to help design an alternative. I was convinced that dentists would gladly dump such a heavy, painful, and unpleasant thing in favor of something lighter and more comfortable.

Al is a very talented tool and model maker. He made some machined components and wax molds for the film holder. He painstakingly worked with the plastic, hand-tooling our designs. The part that held an aiming ring at one end, outside the patient's mouth, and X-rays at the other end, inside the mouth, was relatively easy to construct. But the X-ray film holder required more trial and error. We tried various degrees of stiffness; some were too soft, some too hard. We went through four or five generations of our design, giving our samples to a dentist to try with his patients. The dentist would tell us if a part was too hard to move, if the bites were soft enough for patient comfort, what parts a dentist needed to be able to sterilize, and if the material we'd given him withstood autoclaving (high-temperature sterilization).

We minimized the part count in comparison with the existing X-ray devices and wound up with a reusable aiming ring and calibrated indicator beam that could be autoclaved, and individually wrapped disposable bites. Because we used mostly lightweight medical-grade polymers in its construction, the tool was ultra light. We got patent protection and called it the Kanbar Target.

When we were satisfied that we had a good design, we made a mold so that we could produce fifty samples and give them to dentists. We expected them to fall in love with the Target, place reorders, and spread the word about our wonderful innovation.

The Kanbar Target was an excellent product that met all the criteria we set for it. So why didn't it fly off the shelves? What happened to those reorders?

It didn't sell because the Target solved the patients' problems, not the dentists' problems, and it's the dentists who buy X-ray devices. Dentists don't have a problem with heavier devices. They may not even be aware of their patients' discomfort. What's more, dentists didn't want to purchase disposable, single-use bites. The dentist who helped us design the Target thought it was great, but in retrospect we should have talked to more dentists. There simply isn't enough added value for the actual consumer: the dentist.

We had a hard time finding distributors and making sales, and eventually X-ray technology went fully digital so there is no longer any need for the Target at all. As a business venture, it always operated at a loss, something I was able to accommodate because of my other successes. But all too often, inventors put all their resources into projects such as this, and if they lose, they lose everything.

## THE ROLLOCANE

I also invented the ROLLOcane, a cane-like device with three soft wheels in a tripod arrangement. It provides better support than a regular cane and is far less obtrusive than a walker. We used my mother as a test subject and in the end she loved it, likening it to a comforting "shoulder to lean on." We went into production but only saw modest sales. Medical professionals objected to the fact that its height is not adjustable, and some wished that we'd included brakes. Despite the fact that it is perfectly safe and won't roll out from under a user, the wheels frighten some people.

We should have made prototypes, taken them to nursing homes and physical therapists, and listened long and hard to the feedback we got. We would have discovered that there was indeed a market for a rolling cane, but also that it would need to be adjustable and perhaps have brakes. We haven't taken the time to revamp and either re-launch or license the ROLLOcane because we have so many other front-burner projects.

These three stories highlight two important lessons inventors must learn if they want to find not just monetary success in the marketplace, but also an eager, appreciative audience for innovations.

- *First, correctly identify the customers for your product, and understand exactly what they want and need and how they'll use it.*

- *And second, build a prototype and test your invention with its potential users so you can identify mistakes and pitfalls and correct them before you take your product to market.*


## TWO POPSICLE STICKS AND A COAT HANGER: PROVE YOUR INVENTION CHEAPLY AND SIMPLY

I have an inventor friend who says that if you can, you should prove your invention with nothing more elaborate than two Popsicle sticks and a coat hanger. The idea for folding aircraft wings, so important for saving space on an aircraft carrier, was conceptualized using a bent paper clip and a rubber eraser. In other words, your first model should be inexpensive and

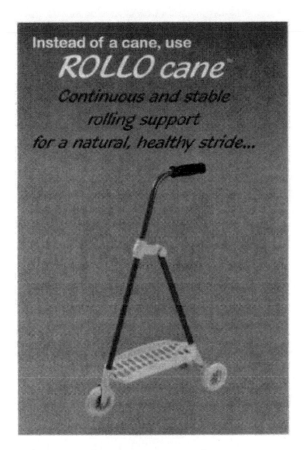

Instead of a cane, use
*ROLLO cane*
*Continuous and stable
rolling support
for a natural, healthy stride...*

rudimentary. In some cases, in order to prove your idea will work, or to get financial backing or a licensing deal, draftsman-quality drawings will suffice. And remember, the Patent Office doesn't require a working model.

Depending on your invention, you will probably develop a succession of more elaborate and accurate prototypes as you refine your ideas and test them with end users. Prototyping typically goes through some or all of these phases:

+ **Basic Design.** *In working out the general shape of your invention, you may wind up with something nonfunctional or something that functions crudely. This early design probably won't be made of the material you ultimately envision, as was the case with my homemade D-Fuzz-It®.*

- **Functional Model.** *This one is tested until it works as you'd like (the various Kanbar Targets generated in our lab).*

- **Model Modified Based on Testing.** *This is tested on end-users and improved.*

- **Working Prototype.** *Ideally, this is tested by actual consumers in a real-world (not laboratory) setting (for example, the Targets we gave to a dentist).*

- **Production Models.** *These are sold in a test market. (Adapted from DeMatteis 1997, pp. 32-33.)*

Many basic or merely functional prototypes can be made at home. By this I don't mean that you should learn to work with injection-molded plastics or metal casting in your garage, or dive right into CAD (although to some extent you can); I mean that you should not invest thousands of dollars paying a manufacturer to do these things in your earliest prototyping phases. To begin, you need to prove to yourself that your idea is feasible, and depending on your end user and market, you may want to create something you can test out informally on a few sample consumers. Not every invention lends itself easily to a rough working model: I couldn't make a tiny Quad cinema and run a few films to see if people showed up—though I have read that in developing their Courtyard hotel chain, the Marriott Corporation built a prototype room with movable walls in order to test various possible designs (Thomas 1995, p. 214). Extremely technical or idea-based inventions—like software—are difficult to model effectively without creating a nearly final product, or without using computerized design tools (which I will talk about in the next section). On the other hand, we can envision our fictional Mary prototyping her intermittent wiper with a wiper unit she bought at a junkyard, bolted to a rough wooden base and powered by a 12-volt transformer.

When starting out, you want to keep things as simple and inexpensive as possible because you don't want to throw good money at model makers or manufacturers for the execution of a bad idea. Injection-molding plastic, for instance, can be quite costly. If you spend a small fortune perfecting a finely polished first model, you are more apt to forget the Eleventh Commandment—Thou Shalt Not Bullshit Thyself—and ignore the complaints and red flags that come up in its testing. You may become blind to its faults. Just as hundreds of patents exist for unmarketable inventions (the Kanbar Target was patented), countless models of valueless ideas exist. If you spend thousands on a production-tooled model and then find it needs substantial modifications, you may have to scrap that expensive model and begin again. But when you do it cheaply you are free to make mistakes and start over.

If Popsicle sticks and coat hangers won't prove your invention, consider using clay, wood, plastic, fabric, vinyl, sheet metal or even cast metal.

Clay is great for making molds for a plastic or metal model. There are also polymer clays available in arts and crafts stores that are pliable, like clay, yet hard and durable after being baked.

Epoxy putty can be used similarly to clay, but it has the advantage of curing extremely hard and being highly adhesive.

Wood can simulate plastic or metal. Balsa wood (available in hobby shops) works well if you need to shape parts. You can ask for help, or find an inexpensive helper, at a woodworking or model airplane shop.

Plastic? You can try this at home. It's not brain surgery—bending plastic over an electric stove is easy—but you do need to educate yourself about techniques, materials, tools and safety. Plastic suppliers, hobby shops and art supply stores carry liquid plastic resins that can be molded in simple handmade molds, and sheet plastics that can be cut, bent and glued. Visit some stores and ask questions.

Many fabric or vinyl models can be made on a home sewing machine.

Sheet metal is relatively inexpensive and can be used to demonstrate something that will ultimately be made of plastic. If you take a crude cardboard mock-up to a sheet metal fabricator, he or she can create a good, cheap prototype.

Cast-metal objects can be simulated with custom castable plastics. Kits and compounds are available from outfits such as Castolite (see appendix).

Special metal alloys are available that will melt at very low temperatures, so you can make a mold out of clay or even paper.

Many models require some machining—drilling, punching, shaping, planing and so on. If you have the equipment, you can do this yourself. If not, take your model to a machine shop or enlist the help of a hobbyist. A hand-held motor tool like those in the Dremel® line enables you to cut, carve, drill, polish, and grind with ease.

## SOME PROTOTYPING RESOURCES

- *EBay and Craigslist for second-hand or new parts and machinery. There are countless other online resources.*

- *Builders of model airplanes and other hobbyists can talk to you about the technology you need, or perhaps make your prototype at a low price.*

- *California Manufacturing Technology Center is a state agency that helps inventors develop their inventions. Other states may have similar programs.*

- Fine Scale Modeler, Design News, Machine Design, Gizmag, and Popular Mechanics *magazines for articles and supplier ads.*

- Make Magazine *is dedicated to the "maker" community. Also a great source of ideas and supplier ads.*

- *McCaster-Carr Supply Company (Los Angeles, CA), for a staggering assortment of tools and hardware*

- The Modelmaker's Handbook *(Alfred A. Knopf)*

- *Harbor Freight Tools sells a wide variety of low-cost tools.*

- *Micro-Mark, "The Small Tool Specialists."*

- *Electronics surplus stores. I've seen a number of these that sell affordable electronic components, motors, gears, tools, and raw materials. The Surplus Center (www.surpluscenter.com) has a wide variety of industrial-strength parts, including electronic, pneumatic and hydraulic components, motors, gear drives and more.*

· *United States Plastic Corporation and TAP Plastics sell plastic materials, glues, and tools.*

For details on all of these, and other resources, look them up online or see the appendix.

If you know of a part or product that is similar to what you want to create, consider contacting the manufacturer to see if any old or discontinued molds are available. You might be able to have that mold machined to suit your need. Cannibalized parts—handles, nozzles, switches and the like—taken from existing products can often work beautifully. These can be obtained cheaply at flea markets, garage sales and discount stores (Debelak 1997, pp. 133-45).

## THE DIGITAL REVOLUTION IN PROTOTYPING

Digitization has changed everything and building the prototype of your invention is no exception. Advanced computer aided design (CAD) software enables anyone from home tinkerers to senior engineers to design the parts of their inventions solely within the memory of a computer and to test how they fit and function together. The CAD file can then direct computerized machinery to create a real-world object. Even the average person inventing something at home can benefit from the huge cuts in time and expense that the two primary computer-driven prototyping techniques—CNC machining and 3D printing—can provide.

## CNC MACHINING

Computer numerical control (CNC) machining has been available for decades both as a prototyping tool and a production line tool. Any shape that can be modeled in three dimensions on a computer can be reproduced relatively easily and very accurately via CNC. With a finished CAD file, computer-controlled milling machines, lathes, laser cutters, sewing machines, welders, plasma cutters and other machines will cut, fasten, carve, bend, shape, stitch, mold, assemble and otherwise manipulate metal, plastic, wood, ceramics, composites, fabrics and practically any other construction material known to man.

CNC machining is similar to traditional techniques in that it starts with a large hunk of material and cuts away whatever is not needed. This is called "subtractive manufacturing."[1] There's a lot of waste, it's time consuming, and errors are expensive to correct. CNC can handle large heavy objects with speed and precision so if you're inventing something like a new car suspension then CNC may be right for you. If you need a lot of one thing produced, CNC can do it with greater efficiency, consistency and precision than many other methods.

## 3D PRINTING

A few years after selling off SKYY, I began production of Blue Angel Vodka. I wanted something really eye catching for displaying Blue Angel bottles in bars. Al Kolvites and I came up with an idea for a small translucent plastic display base with flashing LEDs. The bottle would sit in the socket of this cone-shaped base and the LEDs would catch the bar patrons' attention. We sketched it up and Al went away. About a day later he came back with our prototype and we went to show it to a bartender. He said he wouldn't use it because it was too wide and would crowd out other bottles from his shelf. So Al went back to his workshop and later that day came back with a narrower version. The bartender loved it. After that we made a few minor changes and sent the files off to have a mold made for injection molding. The flashing LED unit is a commercially available warning flasher for bicycles. How's that for re-using an existing product?

This rapid prototyping was made possible through the magic of three-dimensional printing. I think 3D printing is about the best prototyping tool for the small inventor since the X-Acto® Knife because of its speed, small footprint and relatively low cost. In my opinion it's more accurate to name it 3D model making, but I'll call it 3D printing because that's what everyone else says.

3D printing uses a computer-controlled machine to build up a three

dimensional object out of raw materials. Currently, some of the best low-end printers spray out millions of micro-dots of melted plastic, layer upon layer, and they make a very smooth finished product. Different 3D printers use varying deposition techniques and produce different levels of quality, strength, and precision. Some can print with metal and some in other materials. Price varies significantly in the cost of the machines and the per-piece cost of the objects they create.

With 3D printing you can build up a prototype from a CAD file very quickly and with little waste. Two iterations of the same product used to take a month but we finalized that bottle base in two days. 3D printing is showing few limitations, and has been used to create "everything from simple chess pieces to more complex objects such as functioning clocks."[2] One company in San Francisco is using it to create highly customized prosthetic limbs.[3] Bre Pettis, CEO of MakerBot® Industries, LLC, said, "We created MakerBot to help innovators iterate faster, more affordably and (to help them) invent more."[4] MakerBot produces a line of relatively inexpensive 3D printers targeted at the general public.

If your final product will be made of ceramic, metal, wood, or something else, go ahead and "print" in plastic in 3D. Carve it, sand it, drill it, glue it and build it up with epoxy until you get the shape right. Adjust your CAD file to match and print a new prototype. Or have your final version scanned in three dimensions and converted to CAD files for machining or molding. 3D printing is ideal for small items, but if your prototype is large then traditional fabrication methods may be more economical.

You can buy your own 3D printer sized to fit on your desk. Some kits are available for around $500, or you could spend tens of thousands. Popular models currently range from $2,000 to $4,000. I'm not going to bother listing them here because by the time you read this they will all have changed and new options will be available. Remember that you will also need compatible CAD software and the skill to run it.

3-D printing is currently seen as a disruptive force that will turn manufacturing on its ear. This is explored a bit in Chapter 4, "Manufacture or License?"

## GETTING HELP WITH COMPUTER-DRIVEN PROTOTYPING

If you're a hands-on, nuts-and-bolts, build-it-yourself person like I am, don't worry. Simple inventions and brainstorming are often faster and easier to do in the home workshop with manual techniques. Even a complex organic shape you mold by hand out of clay can be scanned in three dimensions and turned into a CAD file for CNC machining or 3D printing.

There are freelance designers who could work up your CAD files. Local machine shops may be equipped with CNC machines and 3D printing services are popping up all over. Check online or in your phone book for local professionals and shops.

If you want to do it yourself but are frustrated at a lack of experience and/or access to tools, check out TechShop™ at http://www.techshop.ws. This is one of the greatest developments I have ever seen for the individual inventor. You pay for membership and get access to a wide variety of machine tools (including 3D printers), software, and the basic training to use them.[5] They have several locations around the U.S. with more on the way. Anton Willis prototyped his Oru™ folding kayak at TechShop.

Anything that requires a lot of iterations to get right, or something that requires great precision will benefit from using digital design during prototyping. A digital model can be copied, manipulated and changed very quickly, like any other computer file. Once you make a mold, correcting errors is expensive and difficult because you have to modify the mold. So do as much as you can on computer files and cheap 3D printing before you make your first mold. When it comes to production, it can save you days, weeks, or even months in tooling up because your prototype's digital files may be useful in programming production line machines.

In my opinion, how you create the prototype is secondary to the reasons you create the product, the way you protect it and how you market it. The current digital revolution in prototyping has more to do with savings in cost and time during development than with creating a better, more useful product. A useful product still has to come from your own head. After all, a computer can't decide what will solve a customer's problem or choose the perfect shade of blue for a vodka bottle.

## INEXPENSIVE PROTOTYPING ALTERNATIVES

If you find you do need professional assistance, there are still ways to get low-cost prototypes. If you can get orders for your invention using drawings, a homemade model and good salesmanship, you may be able to convince a manufacturer to pay for a final working prototype in exchange for your future business. You will need to sell the manufacturer on the merits and moneymaking potential of your idea.

At local businesses, you can seek out an industrial designer, machinist or model maker willing to moonlight and build your prototype at cost in return for a share of your future profits. And consider contacting the design department of your local college. You might find a student or professor you can employ cheaply. If you work with an outside resource like a machine shop or CAD designer, make sure to get them to sign your NDA (nondisclosure agreement).

The Good Grips™ people produced hundreds of testing models by carving Styrofoam and wood. In developing their salad spinner, simple 2D sketches and 3D volumetric foam mock-ups were used. They also used CAD to create dimensionally accurate models. I invented a surgical instrument to be used by doctors in treating varicose veins—smaller, less invasive than the state-of-the-art technology at the time—and licensed it to Johnson & Johnson. After crafting a handmade sample, I invested in an inexpensive aluminum mold that could make a number of samples, so that I would have a working prototype to show potential licensees. (These days I might have used 3D printing, depending on the number I needed.) For reasons we'll explore in greater depth when we discuss licensing, I've found a finished product to be very advantageous when pitching, much more persuasive than even the best drawings.

Because I had made a mold, I could easily provide Johnson & Johnson with 150 samples. They test-marketed these samples, getting a great response and paving the way for our deal. The extent to which you develop your invention—whether you stop at precision drawings or continue on to production models—will depend on many things. What is customary in the field in which your invention will be competing? Can you license with drawings or a crude model? Can you write an accurate patent application before having developed a working prototype? Are you manufacturing and distributing on your own, or is licensing your goal? How many building skills and how much development money do you have? There are no hard and fast, across-the-board rules—except the need to prove that your idea can be turned into an invention that is marketable.

Finally, because it bears repeating: Keep it simple. This pertains both to making prototypes and to your ideas. The best inventions promise and exemplify simplicity in their function and design. What could be simpler than the Chip Clip? A key selling point of Macintosh® computers has always been their easy set-up. My friend Knud Dyby was told by an injection molder that his invention was too simple to warrant a patent. He had taken a plastic box and put a ring-shaped magnet on a hole at the top and used it to store and dispense paper clips. The elegant simplicity of his idea and its execution could have made him millions if he had sought a patent. There's no such thing as too simple.

## MONEY, MONEY, MONEY, MONEY, MONEY!

While your first step after getting an idea shouldn't be mortgaging the house, some things do require cold hard cash. It's not true that you need a lot of money to make a lot of money—having resources can sometimes make it easy to be wasteful and imprudent—but, of course, having ready access to development funds doesn't hurt. Most of us, though, need help funding the prototype for our invention and, more importantly, funding its manufacture. Getting this start-up capital can be a daunting task and is almost an art in itself. It's beyond the scope of this book to describe fully the complicated world of raising money, but I can point you in some solid directions.

At this point in the development process, many people are attracted to those inventor's services companies that promise to take care of all kinds of bothersome details for you so that you can sit back and wait for royalty checks to arrive in the mail. Beware.

> *Making the complicated simple, awesomely simple, that's creativity.*
>
> **CHARLES MINGUS**

Invention assistance outfits rarely provide real help. It's in their best interest to tell you they have "researched" your idea and found it to be a guaranteed moneymaker. By doing so, they hope to persuade you to further invest in their "services." They will find you a model maker all right—if you send them a fat check. (Services that insist you first get a patent and then offer to present your invention to a variety of manufacturers are more likely to be legit.) You can't do everything yourself and you don't have to, but you should take charge. Learn to do what you can and learn all about what you hire others to do so that you can employ them intelligently.

> *Money helps, though not so much as you think when you don't have it.*
>
> **LOUISE ERDRICH,** *THE BINGO PALACE*

When you do need to raise money, there are a number of ways to go. When a plastic mold maker said he wanted $1,200 to make a mold and prototype of my D-Fuzz-It®, I went to friends, family and business associates and offered them a piece of the pie. If they provided start-up funds, they could get in on the ground floor and take a percentage of the business. Pity for them, most said no. But I did ultimately go into business with one friend who invested some initial packaging and marketing funds. Many, if not most, inventors find they need to make similar deals in order to realize their plans. The less developed your idea, the bigger the risk your partner or partners are taking and thus the greater percentage you're likely to need to offer them.

When I wanted to produce and market SKYY® Vodka, I had adequate personal financial resources to do so. But I honestly believe that if I were twenty-nine years old, with the SKYY® idea and no money, I could still have launched the product by giving 40% or even 50% of the business to investors. If you're a lousy pitch person, hire someone to pitch your product to investors or offer the pitch person a percentage of future earnings. When I was getting ready to launch my Tangoes® game, I happened to meet a young salesman, Mark Chester, at a party. We had a great conversation and I was impressed by his hard "soft sell." I told him about my game, asked if he'd like to try to sell it in area stores, and he gave it a shot. Mark did well and said he'd like to represent the product. I said, "Fantastic!" because I wasn't interested in making sales or running the

Tangoes® business. I told Mark he could have the first $20,000 the game brought in and offered him an 80/20 split from there on out. We went on to become partners in the successful Tangoes® business.

In raising money, as in inventing, you are only limited by your imagination. Approach the task as you would an inventing problem. Be creative. If you have a novel idea about how to approach someone or what kind of deal to make, don't dismiss it outright. Think it through, protect yourself with simple contracts and legal advice if need be, and then go for it.

There are almost infinite variations of the classic I-invent/you-put-up-the-money deal. As mentioned earlier, you can often trade a small percentage of your future business for designing, tooling or manufacturing services. Distribution channel financing is another option: you get up-front money for signing a distribution agreement with a larger company.

Baby Jogger® inventor Phil Baechler and his wife, Mary, kept their day jobs and went through their $8,000 personal savings while building custom strollers in their garage. Though their strollers were selling, they had trouble finding investors—but they didn't quit. With a "patent pending" and the last of their cash, they placed an ad in Runner's World, incorporated Racing Strollers, Inc., and started selling mail order. Happy customers and free publicity generated by Phil's press releases helped the company grow quickly. By the time the patent was issued a few years later, sales were impressive enough for them to finally secure an operating line of credit and a development loan from the Small Business Administration (SBA) to build a real factory. You can make use of the SBA as well, and your local chamber of commerce should also be able to direct you to local business assistance offices.

What about banks? Banks will lend you money if you have a track record and they believe you can pay them back. Lending money is their business, but banks are inherently conservative. And backing yourself up on paper for a bank can be difficult. It's harder to write a convincing business plan for new inventions because you are dealing with something new and there are many unknowns. Obviously, you have reason to believe in the sales potential, but banks generally want much more hard data than you can provide. Banks don't want to be venture capitalists, and most small businesses can't meet their tight loan requirements.

## SOME FINANCING RESOURCES

- *Kickstarter.com—see below.*

- *National Association of Small Business Investment Companies*

- *The Small Business Development Center (SBDC) nearest you (for state sources of funding) and the Small Business Administration. Your local Certified Development Corporation can help you prepare your application for government-backed loans.*

- *Small Business Innovation Research awards grants for areas of interest to the Departments of Defense, Health and Human Services, Agriculture, Transportation, Education, and the Interior; NASA; the EPA; the DOE; the National Science Foundation; and the Nuclear Regulatory Commission. Requirements are rigorous.*

- *See the appendix for contact information.*

Kickstarter.com is a funding phenomenon made possible only through Internet technology. It's a "crowdsourcing" tool, where money is pooled from people scattered far and wide and brought together through the website. Someone with a creative project that needs funding can solicit money on the Kickstarter site and their friends, family, and, often, complete strangers pay online via credit card. Recent high-profile Kickstarter projects include a 3D printing pen[6] that made headlines in February 2013 and the Oru folding kayak.[7] The creators of both the PrintBot and the Form1 3-D printers funded their businesses through Kickstarter.[8] The enormous advantage of Kickstarter is that it harnesses an army of small contributors who may each have only a small sum to contribute, rather than forcing you to find one or two big investors.

And what about those venture capitalists? Were they all just "New Economy" whiz kids, and has the Great Recession driven them extinct? Not at all. Anyone can be considered a venture capitalist if they give you money for a share of your business. They can be friends or relations, business associates, local businesspersons, former employers or angels—that is, private, part-time investors. And although money is definitely scarcer than it once was, there are still people out there looking for good places to invest that are not reliant upon a bipolar stock market.

Some resources for finding venture capital include:

- *Pratt's Guide to Venture Capital Sources*

- *Publications such as American Venture Magazine and Entrepreneur*

- *FinanceHub.com (www.financehub.com), information and resources for entrepreneurs and investors*

Management consultant Edwin E. Bobrow points out that "...venturing is the hardest way for an inventor to launch a new product." Licensing is much easier (and is discussed in Chapter 4). Bobrow also stresses that venture capitalists look for the promise of "great management." They "invest in people, not technologies and not products." (Bobrow 1997, pp. 242, 244) This is true, in one form or another, for anyone who might become your partner in business or an investor in your invention.

## MANAGEMENT

While we're on the topic let's look at a few elements of management that, if done well, can really be of help to the new inventor.

## WRITE A BUSINESS PLAN

While an excellent product is a prerequisite, the way to convince people that you know what you're talking about and have the necessary organizational and management savvy to pull it off is to create a business plan, a well-thought-out, researched and documented case for your product and its market. In your business plan, you need to evaluate your product realistically, assess its market and market appeal, and project potential market share, costs and sales. It's like building a working prototype of your invention, and just as vital. You write a business plan to prove to yourself, and then to others, that the product is real, that it's worth producing and that you'll be able to sell it to someone, preferably lots of someone's. Just as the prototype tests your idea with potential customers, the business plan sells it to potential investors. And whatever else it contains, it must convey your viability as a smart manager, organizer, planner and thinker.

## BUSINESS PLAN RESOURCES

- *How to Write a Business Plan (Nolo Press)*

- *The Small Business Administration*

- *Your First Business Plan (Small Business Source Books)*

- *See the appendix for more information*

## MAKE IT GOOD FOR THE BUYER

People don't pay for something unless they see some benefit in the transaction for themselves. It's up to you to demonstrate that benefit to your potential buyers, whether they are consumers, purchasing managers, doctors, the government, or anyone else. One time I overheard one of my salesmen on the phone say to a prospect, "If you buy a hundred cases it'll make my month." I'm telling you right now, the buyer doesn't give a damn about "making your month." She has to make her own month. You have to convince her that your product will help her sell more to her customers, save money, solve problems, help more patients, improve processes, reduce overhead, keep customers happy, or whatever else it is your gizmo is intended to do. This reaches all the way back to product conceptualization. If you create something that people will want or need it will be easier to make a convincing sales pitch. You have to believe in the product you are selling. If I didn't believe in my product I couldn't sell anything. Your prospective customers will pick up on your conviction, they will trust you more, and they will be more likely to buy.

**GET YOUR HANDS DIRTY: SELL IN PERSON**

The importance of building trust cannot be overstated. Humans are still humans (despite the Internet) and they still respond best to a personal touch, such as you handing them one of your products and demonstrating how it works. They want to know they are dealing with a real person and not an email autoresponder. Get in touch with the person who makes purchasing decisions. Give them free samples. Let them try it themselves. Have them put one out where people can see, touch and use it. They will appreciate your willingness to put yourself and your product in the line of fire.

This kind of selling used to be the default. It's still extremely valid today. It's very difficult to gain someone's trust through email or a website, so for creating those initial sales when your product is new, for building some excitement when you are first starting out, for showing how it works and how convenient it is, there is nothing to beat personal contact. The Internet and social media are great to augment this and to stay in touch with existing customers once you have some momentum (see Chapter 5). But recent generations of business managers rely on their computers too much. They seem unwilling to do the legwork that builds those initial relationships and they place too much reliance in online forms and placing bids and sending pitch letters. When you have no brand yet, this just makes you as anonymous as every other supplier. Good management is not about sitting back in your cushy office and directing others to do things. To properly manage a new venture you have to be ready to do whatever is necessary to reach your target market, or to develop a niche market. See Chapter 5 to see how we built an extremely solid grassroots marketing campaign for SKYY®.

**ADVERTISING IS OVER-HYPED**

Nowadays marketers like to get a chunk of money and spend it on an expensive ad campaign. Ads don't work that well for a lot of products. Audiences are inundated with advertising and the message is often totally lost. Ads are good for building brand recognition, but if you don't have a strong brand yet the message may fall flat. I advertise very little for any of my products. I prefer to spend marketing money on more focused, personalized efforts to crack open niche markets.

## PEOPLE WATCHING: OBSERVE THE END USER

To prove that you have a launch-worthy product, you need to conduct clearheaded research of your market and ruthlessly review your invention at every step. Depending on your product and your personality, you might want to do the bulk of this analysis and research at the beginning, when all you have is an idea, or you might wait until after you've built a basic prototype, but it must be done before making large financial outlays. If you're funding your own efforts, don't think you can skip this process, as it's vital to your ultimate success. And if you're looking to others for start-up funds, anyone except perhaps an indulgent relative with deep pockets is going to expect you to gather this data and put it into a coherent, convincing document.

Al's previous employer, InterMetro, had an almost unbelievable success rate for their new products. Something like nine out of ten of them went on to make money. The national average is one out of ten. What made them so special?

They followed a process, very much like the Five Fundamental Steps in this book, and made certain that market, consumer and design needs were aligned. Marketing defined the need for a product, proving that a new product was needed to fill a void or that a much-improved version was needed to meet and beat the competition. InterMetro's industrial design department researched and defined what the product had to be to meet or exceed the customer's expectations. The engineering department worked with industrial design to ensure that the product could be profitably manufactured while meeting consumer needs. Their constant vigilance to reconcile all of these needs ensured that the company was never in the position of trying to convince customers that InterMetro had produced what they wanted. Instead they produced exactly what customers needed.

To find out what the consumer wants and needs, do market research.

And by this I don't mean focus groups and the kind of pie charts and graphs consultants charge a small fortune for. If focus groups worked, the big companies would never put out products that fail, which they do all the time as I illustrated with the Coke and Pepsi low-sugar colas. Guy Kawasaki faults focus groups because unlike real life, they "are clean." In them, "participants project how they would use a product— sitting comfortably in a room with other people listening to them, with conversation facilitated by a professional, and feeling like they have to express an opinion since they've been paid to be in the group." (Kawasaki 1999, p. 50) My theory is that focus groups are used by executives to cover their tracks—when their products flop they can slap their hands to their foreheads in bewilderment and say, "But we had the numbers!"

Kawasaki also says that "since nothing is more important than gathering information about your customers ... you should never leave it to marketing research professionals." He contends that their methods are unable to detect and communicate subtle findings, they miss unforeseen opportunities, they provide stale information because of the time it takes to make all those pie charts and as a consequence, they let crucial issues fall through cracks. (Kawasaki 1999, pp. 115-16) You must see for yourself, on the customer's turf, what the problem you think you are solving really is.

Much of the market research you might pay for will give you composite portraits of potential buyers based on averages. But averages that are supposed to please everyone usually wind up pleasing no one. I was hosting a dinner party one evening, and when it came time for coffee, naturally some guests asked for regular and some wanted decaf. After a sleepless night, I queried my housekeeper about her coffee preparation the night before. She explained she had brewed half a pot of regular coffee, half a pot of decaf, and then mixed them together. "I thought half-and-half would make everyone happy," she explained. I wasn't 50% happy, I was 100 % annoyed! I should have remembered this lesson when brewing up 80/20 cola.

So what kind of market research do you have to do? It really comes down to talking to and observing your end user, your potential customers, and assessing the market they create.

## LOW-COST MARKET RESEARCH

- *Use the Internet. Listen in or "lurk" in chat rooms, discussion boards, LinkedIn groups, Facebook, and other places online where consumers go to talk about consumer products, or where professionals go to discuss their industry. Post your own questions to steer discussion threads in a way that will get them talking about your area of interest.*

- *Set up a poll or questionnaire on Facebook, LinkedIn or your blog. Ask two or three key questions. Invite people from chat rooms and other online discussion venues to participate. Watch out for "trolls." Some people like to stir things up online by intentionally providing false or inflammatory answers.*

- *Test your reasoning, not necessarily your idea, on people you know will be absolutely honest with you. ("Would you buy a gadget that quickly and easily removed sweater pills?" not "How would you feel about a sweater comb?")*

- *Approach people who work in the market you are trying to enter and offer to pay them for a few hours of consulting time. Again, you need not disclose your idea. Ask about existing products, consumer feedback, and any unusual sales factors.*

- *Talk to distributors, storeowners and salespeople.*

- *Go to trade shows.*

The phrase "the customer is always right" is not an unfounded truism: customers vote yea or nay with their dollars. If they vote nay for any reason—a single feature of your product is discouraging or unwanted, the product looks undistinguished on the shelves, the product isn't sold in the places customers expect to find it—only you and your invention lose. You must involve them in your process, learning more about them than even they know about themselves.

Begin by going where your end users live, work and shop. If you'd like to see your product sold at Wal-Mart, go to Wal-Mart. Talk to people buying items similar to yours. They are the ideal focus group. Talk to the people who sell items similar to yours; they can give you information on what sells well for them, and what might sell even better. Anton Willis had friends, strangers, novices, and experienced kayakers paddle his Oru™ kayak in everything from flat water to ocean surf, and incorporated their suggestions.[9] And remember my experience with the Kanbar Target: make sure you correctly identify who your real customer is. In some cases, the ones who buy your product are not the same ones who use it directly, and you need to please the people who actually buy. If you hope to get picked up by a distributor, also talk to distributors; you need to convince them first that they want your product before you will have a hope of convincing the end user.

Some inventors get nervous at the mere thought of talking about their invention to anybody, much less with lots of people. "They'll steal my idea," they think. The fear of having your idea stolen must not outweigh the need to test your product out on people. In reality, the chances of someone stealing your idea are much lower than the chances of making an inferior, doomed product because you didn't talk to your customers first.

You've got to consider the opinions of store buyers as well—if they can't be convinced of the uniqueness of your product, you'll never get it on the shelf. I designed the sleek, easy-to-use SKYY® Timer as a promotional giveaway item. People who received this small, digital, magnet-backed timer found it terrifically simple to use and quite handy. I explored the possibility of selling it as a stand-alone item, sans the SKYY® logo, but retail buyers didn't see the need for another timer among the many in the marketplace, and weren't interested in stocking it. The timer solved my problem of needing a nice SKYY® promotional item beautifully, but the retail world didn't perceive a customer need for it.

Not that giveaways can't be turned into great products. S.O.S® steel wool soap pads were created by door-to-door salesman Edwin W. Cox as a way to get his foot in the door to sell kitchenwares. They quickly became more popular than his pots and pans. Same with Avon, which began when door-to-door book salesman David McConnell started to give away small bottles of perfume to people who listened to his pitch. Unfortunately, I should have assessed the timer market and consumer much more thoroughly before deciding to package and sell my giveaway. (Panati 1987, pp. 102, 243-44)

Also, it's not enough to talk to people; you have to watch them buying and using similar products. Often, end users can't articulate what they want, but if you watch them, you can recognize their needs and offer them something they didn't even know they needed, something that will prompt them to say, "How did you know? That's exactly what I could use."

For example, at InterMetro, the product design and development department was given the task of designing a new dish dolly, the piece of

> *Better to ask twice than lose your way once.*
> **DANISH PROVERB**

equipment that holds dishes in stacks in restaurant kitchens. The industrial designer stood in the background and watched the dishwashing process, which in large establishments is done by people and machines. He tried to blend into the background, since if people know they are being watched, they tend to work more conscientiously and mind their manners.

The designer found that the dishes weren't treated very carefully. Workers would bus the dishes, scrape off food scraps, and then load the plates at the front end of the dishwashing machine. Sometimes they'd play a bit of a game with the person unloading dishes at the other end of the machine. The front-end folks would load more dishes on the machine than the unloader could unload. The dishes come off the machine very hot and very fast and need to be stacked. If the machine is overloaded, some poor guy ends up with a huge, unwieldy stack that he literally drops into the dish dolly like a hot potato—not unlike the candy-making episode of I Love Lucy. He can't take the time to gently deposit one dish at a time, and in any case, his fingers won't fit inside the round, plate-shaped hole at the top of the dolly. You can guess the result: lots of cracked and chipped dishes.

The design team introduced a dolly with slots on the sides so that kitchen workers could lower their hands in and deposit, rather than drop, stacks of plates. When they introduced the product at a trade show, competitors were green with envy.

This simple design feature was not the result of consumer requests. When asked what they needed, dishwashers said, "I don't know. Everything is fine as it is." The new design was the result of careful observation.

Assessing the wider, or even national, market is every bit as important as polling individual consumers. I am a big fan of healthy eating, but just because I like my own product does not mean the rest of the world will, as we found out with 80/20 Cola. I am entering the packaged organic foods business with SooFoo™ not for personal reasons but because I've assessed the market for such a thing and I think SooFoo™ is highly viable.

I've assessed the growing desire of the U.S. populace for cleanly grown organic foods. People are eager to "buy American" so SooFoo™ is grown and packaged in the U.S. The vegan market is expanding, including vegan restaurants. I've taken into consideration the fact that people are busy and they don't want to spend a lot of time making their meals and since SooFoo™ is ideally prepared in a rice cooker, it is very low labor. People want to cook up a lot of one dish and have leftovers for several meals, and SooFoo™ can be prepared and eaten plain or combined with any number of other favorites to create interesting meals. Doctors are telling Americans to increase their fiber intake and SooFoo™ is high in fiber, protein and nutrients. You can cook it no-fat, low-fat, or even high-fat, however you like it. One man cooked it up for his son's breakfast and put a little natural maple syrup on it. The kid loved it!

When assessing your market, don't be afraid of targeting a niche, which is simply a small, discrete segment of a large market. The average grocery shopper may not just pick up a package of SooFoo™ and toss it in their cart, but by creating excitement and demand in a niche market we can eventually stimulate the same excitement and demand in a broader market.

That's why we started promoting to health-conscious grocery buyers, an important and growing niche. Our initial product tastings proved our market liked it. Our next step was to expand vertically, reaching more of the markets that serve this niche. SooFoo™ is now available through chains and independent markets that cater to the health-conscious. Awareness is growing and as I write this, Safeway is planning to put it on its shelves in June of 2014. We also sell online through the soofoo.com website.

I'd also like to say that market forces aside, I believe in the importance of organic farming. The pesticides from factory farming are pumping too many toxins into the environment. Chemical fertilizers are exhausting the soil and reducing the nutritional value of our foods. If marketing SooFoo™ helps solve these two problems and gives people something healthy and delicious to eat then that is a satisfying achievement.

I don't assume I can sell SooFoo™ to everyone, but I do believe that a significant portion of health-food buyers will want it. Bob DeMatteis reminds us that giants like Apple Computer, Honda, and Hewlett-Packard each began by targeting niches in existing high-volume markets. "Virtually every entrepreneurial start-up effort begins as a niche." (DeMatteis 1997, p. 44)

I believed there was a segment of the alcohol-drinking population that would embrace a "cleaner" vodka. I was right, and SKYY® Vodka grew well outside its niche boundaries. If you aim your product and marketing efforts at a relatively small segment of the entire population, you actually increase your chances for larger success. Keeping your focus smaller pays off in several ways: it forces you to specify your appeal, it keeps the bar for success at a more attainable height and it limits your losses if you're slightly off.

Starbucks is another example of a company that successfully exploited its niche first before growing into a national force. In fact, when Starbucks began in 1992, it entered a small and even declining coffee-drinking market. In 1962, 75% of the population drank coffee, but thirty years later only 51.4% did so. (Sounds like the movie-going figures in the seventies, right?) So what was Starbucks thinking? Well, they had done their research and figured out that within that declining market, sales of gourmet coffee were actually growing. They had identified a niche, and an expanding one at that. Starbucks mastermind Howard Schultz didn't try to market to the masses; instead he offered "sophisticates" a superior product. (Thomas 1995, pp. 20-28) The rest is history.

## PLAY BY THE RULES

The data you accumulate becomes your road map. The needs people express to you or that you observe become your product priorities, and the dimensions of the market determine the rules of your game. These rules and priorities become your Ten—or Twenty—Commandments. You break them at your peril. Gathered coherently in a business plan, they prove to potential investors and partners the viability of your invention and its market—and not incidentally your own determination and business savvy. Followed wisely, they more often than not will lead you to success in the marketplace.

Even if you think what people ask for is nutty, you'd better take their requests seriously. Al once worked on a low-pressure steam cooker for professional kitchens. Chefs told him they needed to be able to see inside the steamer while items were cooking. Al didn't get this at all—when cooking with steam, a cooked pea or kernel of corn looks exactly like a partially frozen one. But chefs are accustomed to being able to look in ovens and under lids while cooking. So Al struggled to find a way to put a window in the steamer, which drove him crazy because, of course, windows steam up.

Al eventually worked around the problem. He patented a power-conserving steamer that used only as much power as warranted by its contents. A light let cooks know when cooking power was being called for and when the machine was finished cooking. Reassured by the light as to what was going on inside at any given moment, the cooks no longer felt the need to see inside the steam cooking chamber.

As we've seen, Good Grips™ ergonomic designs and innovations are based on extensive research and interviews. In designing their first product, the swivel peeler, they talked with consumers, chefs and retailers, and studied competitive products. After reviewing their research, they decided upon their necessary criteria: a handle large enough to grip firmly and avoid strain, oval-shaped to prevent the tool from turning in the hand, with a rounded end that fits comfortably in the palm and evenly distributes pressure, and an oversized hole for easy hanging. Meeting all of these criteria paved the way for their success and set the standard for the development of their more than 850 ensuing products.

Conditions in the developing world determined the design and manufacture of my inexpensive glasses. They needed to be practically indestructible because of the rough conditions their future owners experience every day. They also needed snap-in lenses so they could be assembled on the spot. We worked with a mold maker who specialized in glasses. Our need for snap-in lenses was new to him, but after we explained things he modified the mold once or twice until the lenses popped in with reasonable pressure, and stayed in place. He wanted to use his accustomed ABS plastic, but when I scientifically tested a pair by stepping on them, they broke. We used far more flexible polypropylene instead. The lenses are polycarbonate for their light weight and resistance to breakage and scratching. We made them round for ease of manufacture and installation. Frames come in two sizes: adult and youth. There are also pre-assembled reading glasses in standard magnifications. We were not too concerned with looks because utility pushed aesthetics way down the list. They look OK, and their brown color resists showing dirt and wear. With these, form unquestionably follows function. So far, they've been a hit with the folks we've given them to.

My Kanbar Target and ROLLOcane are both examples of the pitfalls of inadequate and incomplete research. For the Target, we did heavy product research but not enough market research; though we created a good product, it was a product aimed at the needs of the wrong person. With ROLLOcane, again, our product design was sound, but we failed to take adequate note of end users' perceptions. Logically, we knew brakes were unnecessary, but consumers would have found them reassuring. There really is no way around this process: you need to learn what your product and market commandments are, and then you have to follow through on every one.

In general I've found that most people don't argue with the need for this kind of research. The hard part for most inventors comes sometime after they've gathered the information and then realize that they must modify their invention. As difficult as it sometimes is, that's the goal of all this research: to get your rude awakenings before spending the money to launch. It can be humbling, infuriating or just plain discouraging to return to the drawing board and rethink your product again and again. This development and prototyping phase can often take a long time, and this is good. It provides you with opportunities to discover unforeseen improvements. Creativity is an ongoing process of learning and adjusting; it's more than just a lightning bolt flash of inspiration.

As you build and test prototypes, you will more than likely have some disappointments, but you could also encounter happy surprises. For instance, Ivory soap didn't always float. Too much air was accidentally whipped into a batch. When consumers raved about the bar that couldn't be lost because it bobbed to the surface, extra whipping became part of Ivory's manufacturing process. (Panati 1987, p. 218) Resist the temptation to gloss over inconvenient doubts or unexpected information in order to expedite your design process. Most product entrepreneurs rework their ideas repeatedly. And if your ruthless review uncovers the unpleasant truth that there is no viable market for your product, move on to your next project.

When I still owned SKYY®, it made sense for me to capitalize on its success by extending the line with a flavored vodka. Friends, customers and colleagues were in fact urging me to do just that. But I resisted doing so until I was satisfied we could offer something better and more unique than the other flavored vodkas on the market. That took time. We spent almost a year perfecting a SKYY® Citrus formula. Getting a distinctive taste, one that couldn't be simply reproduced by a bartender with a lemon or lime, took time. We achieved our goal by experimenting with and ultimately melding lemon, lime, orange, grapefruit, and tangerine. But some early versions were cloudy. More adjusting, more experimenting. It took perseverance and determination to get everything—flavor, appearance and finish—just right, and it took a willingness to wait, trusting that launching an inferior or derivative product early was not as important as launching an excellent and unique product a little later.

We are currently doing that with SooFoo™. Folks want a quick way to make a delicious meal and they like variety. So we now offer SooFoo™ with spices and flavors mixed right in. In addition to Original, we now have Garlic and Herb, Hint of Curry, and Moroccan Medley. We thought long and hard about what kinds of flavors to offer. True to our word, we tried out a bunch of recipes our customers had sent us, and incorporated some of their ideas. Some of our own staff came in with ideas of their own. We cooked up loads of experimental recipes in our test kitchen and had tasting "parties" among the staff. ("Try this one. No? OK, how about this with less curry powder?") Amazingly, most of them still like it. And now we have a more diversified line. We are looking at ways to make it more convenient for customers by selling it pre-cooked in special packaging so it can be microwaved. Customers will gladly pay for this convenience.

My Vermeer Dutch Chocolate Cream liqueur followed a similarly long developmental path. Many years ago, I tasted a popular cream

> *Next in importance to having a good aim is to recognize when to pull the trigger.*
>
> **ELMER G. LETERMAN**

liqueur made with Irish whiskey. I thought I could make a better cream liqueur with premium vodka and chocolate. Of course, I had plenty of experience with premium vodka, but finding the right chocolate proved difficult. When I found the best, a wonderful Dutch chocolate, it was quite costly and I was advised against it. But the Dutch have been making an art of fine chocolate for centuries and deserve their reputation for producing the best in the world. I stood firm and insisted on it. After all, if I intend to make a premium product, and I'm using premium vodka, wouldn't a cheaper chocolate defeat the whole point? Then came a long—and not unenjoyable—process of creating and taste testing various blends. Our end result was worth every bit of time we took to perfect it. The time and trouble you take up front will save you both in the long run. Get it right the first time.

Even if you realize you've made a mistake after going to market, you can still sometimes recover—and learn invaluable lessons in the bargain. Look at General Motors' Saturn; they turned a mistake into a triumph. Despite years of research and development, GM subsidiary Saturn initially faced production problems, a recessionary market and even significant product recalls when it launched in the mid-1980s. But they turned their problems into opportunities and earned a reputation for customer satisfaction. Promptly and honestly identifying and solving problems came to symbolize Saturn's commitment to having happy customers, it became part of their marketing, and it earned them high marks in the J. D. Powers and Associates 1992 survey of customer satisfaction (Thomas 1995, p. 15). GM discontinued the Saturn line in 2010, as a result of drastically altered economic forces, the 2008 market crash and GM's government bailout, but Saturn remains a great historical example of a spectacular recovery after a faltering launch. One of my high-level managers drives an older Saturn to this day.

If you have an invention that you know other people need and want, that you can make profitably and that has a defined market, it's time to protect it.

> *I failed my way to success.*
> **THOMAS EDISON, INVENTOR AND HOLDER OF 1,093 PATENTS**

## (ENDNOTES)

1   http://en.wikipedia.org/wiki/3D_printing

2   http://www.cnn.com/2013/02/13/tech/innovation/obama-3d-printing/index.html?hpt=hp_bn5

3   http://www.nytimes.com/2010/09/14/technology/14print.html?pagewanted=all&_r=0

4   http://www.cnn.com/2013/02/13/tech/innovation/obama-3d-printing/index.html?hpt=hp_bn5

5   http://www.techshop.ws/FAQs.html

6   http://www.businessweek.com/articles/2013-02-20/mind-turns-into-matter-with-3d-printing-pen

7   http://www.wired.com/design/2012/11/oru-folding-kayak/

8   http://www.nytimes.com/2013/02/21/garden/the-3-d-printer-may-be-the-home-appliance-of-the-future.html?hp&_r=0

9   http://www.wired.com/design/2012/11/oru-folding-kayak/

# 3.

# Protect Your Idea
## Better Safe than Sorry:
## The Needle Protector

**M**any years ago my physician, Martin Sturman, showed me a design he'd come up with for a safety needle. Martin is a longtime friend who had earlier put me on the path to inventing SKYY®. Over the years of our friendship, he's seen me invent and license a number of medical devices. Many of these had sprung from casual conversations with doctor friends during which they described how they performed a certain medical procedure. As you can imagine, I always asked a lot of questions and several times went on to invent or improve an instrument.

Martin had observed the need to protect medical personnel, who often experience accidental needle sticks, or "sharps-related injuries." His description of the problem—the frequency with which people are stuck, the dangerous, and sometimes fatal, diseases they can contract through these sticks and the inadequacy of the safety devices of the time—immediately convinced me that this was a problem worth solving.

Back then there were something like 5.6 million healthcare workers in the nation. By checking with the Centers for Disease Control and Prevention, we found that these workers sustained hundreds of thousands of needle stick injuries annually, exposing them to a variety of diseases. Early in 2000, OSHA, the Occupational Safety and Health Administration, issued a Bloodborne Pathogen Compliance Directive aimed at ensuring that healthcare workers have access to safety-engineered sharps devices that reduce their risk of injury and infection. Congressional hearings on the subject followed.

Operating, emergency and patient room care can often be hectic, with several things happening at once, and many people getting in one another's way. Needle sticks have always been a common occupational hazard, but with the virulence of HIV/AIDS, hepatitis C and the like, the stakes were higher than ever. An estimated twelve-thousand medical workers were infected with hepatitis B and HIV annually and at least twenty-nine healthcare workers were documented to have contracted the AIDS virus through needle sticks at work as of 1998. (*San Francisco Chronicle*, April 14, 1998)

Unfortunately, Martin's needle design was inadequate. It was somewhat complicated, using springs and tethers and requiring a longer than normal needle. He had shown his device to Becton, Dickinson and Company (BD), the world's largest manufacturer of medical devices and a pioneer in the development of healthcare safety products. They had rejected it, so Martin asked me to consider the problem.

Existing safety needles required the use of two hands. We talked to nurses, who experience 46% of all sharps injuries, and they told us this was impractical in many situations. They wanted a needle that could be "safed" quickly and with one hand, preferably with one finger.

We also talked to doctors, hospital administrators and purchasing agents. Final decisions are often made by the purchasing department; if it's too expensive, they don't buy it. But it seemed likely to us at the time that legislation was coming that would force the purchase of safety needles, so while we always seek the best way to solve a problem at the lowest cost, we concentrated on the needs of the end user, the nurses. We knew we had conducted enough product research with them when we began to hear the same requests over and over. When you are no longer hearing anything new—but not before then—you know it's time to move on to satisfying those needs.

The best inventions are so simple that in retrospect they seem self-evident. (Remember my story about my friend and his paper clip dispenser? That would have made a spectacular patent.) Al Kolvites, designer Robert Cohn and I perfected a push rod and a cover that locks. After the needle is used, it can be propelled through a hole and into its cap with one finger. The needle is locked in the cap, unable to move back through the hole because the cap is cocked at a slight angle and the needle is no longer aligned with the hole. The locking mechanism clicks into place, letting personnel feel and hear that the needle is safe without even taking their eyes off the patient. Once locked, the hypodermic can be dropped and still not perforate its cap.

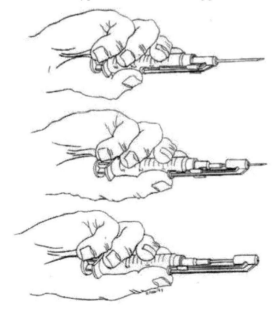

We worked with plastic and Scotch tape first and then cut bits of plastic with a razor knife and melted parts together. Reassured that we were on the right track, we did some precision drawings that further solidified our thinking. When we'd achieved our single-hand push mechanism with an easy bar-and-lock device, we applied for a patent (with an artist's renderings) and invested $10,000 in a one-cavity mold to produce a working model.

We brought the mold to BD and they were impressed. Having a mold that can produce samples, rather than only drawings, which then take a large company months to bureaucratically move through the development stage, always impresses a potential licensee. Because BD is the world's biggest and best manufacturer of medical devices, working with them was our goal. We would never have tried to manufacture and sell a needle protector on our own. BD has the complex machinery needed to mass-produce the needles and a broad, established distribution network. If BD had passed, we would have moved on, showing the product to other medical technology firms.

We (the patent is in the names of all four of us since we each played a creative role in its design) licensed the rights to the patent to BD for an up-front sum and royalties. My top-notch patent attorney, Mike Ebert, also negotiated a minimum yearly payment. This gave BD incentive not to sit on the patent but to produce and distribute the needles quickly. Our agreement also allowed us to take the needle elsewhere if, after a certain period of time, BD had not begun to manufacture and sell them. BD did put our needle on the market, calling it the Safetyglide™ Shielding Injection Needle.

A magazine interviewer once asked me, "What would you invent if you could invent anything in the world?" I answered, "A cure for AIDS." Unfortunately, I'm not equipped to turn that idea into an invention. But according to the CDC website, "sharps-related injuries in nonsurgical hospital settings decreased 31.6% during 2001–2006 (following the Needlestick Safety and Prevention Act of 2000).[1] So maybe I've at least helped prevent a few people from contracting some of these awful diseases.

Solving problems always feels good, as does making an honest buck, but being part of this happy outcome feels especially good.

## THIS WON'T HURT A BIT: UNDERSTANDING PATENTS

The Constitution gives Congress the power "to Promote the Progress of Science and Useful Arts, by securing for limited Times to Authors and inventors the exclusive Right to their respective Writings and Discoveries" (Article 1, Section 8). In exchange for explaining their work and putting it in writing for all to see, inventors typically get exclusive rights for twenty years beginning on the date on which the patent is granted and ending twenty years from the date on which the patent application was filed in the United States[2]. Because of exceptions and extensions some types of patents may have different durations. . Patents issued before 1995 are granted seventeen years of protection from the date the patent was issued. Patents were intended to spur innovation by creating a repository of how-to information. While one cannot make, use or sell a patented invention without risking being sued by the patent owner, one can study the technology behind the patent and perhaps improve upon it. For instance, in June of 1941, actress Hedy Lamarr and composer George Antheil received a patent for a radio-controlled torpedo "Secret Communications System." Though it wasn't used during WW II, after the patent had expired, Sylvania modified the system and applied it to satellite technology.

Only three patents were issued in 1790, the first year they were issued in the United States. The examiners were the Secretary of State, the Secretary of War and the Attorney General. In 2010, the United States

---

### SOME NAMES AND DATES (THERE WILL BE NO QUIZ!)

- 1421-History's first recorded patent for an industrial invention is granted to Filippo Brunelleschi, in Florence, Italy.
- 1641-The first American colonial patent is issued, in Massachusetts, for a salt-making process.
- 1790-The first U.S. patent is issued, for a new method of making pearl ash and potash for fertilizer.

Patent and Trademark Office (USPTO) granted more than 132,000 patents[3] and approximately 5,588,000 patents were issued globally.[4] Today's somewhat lesser titled examiners are specialists in various aspects of technology, charged with being well versed in the "prior art," or prior developments and concepts, in their area of expertise.

Examiners review a patent application with respect to three main criteria: The invention must be (1) useful, (2) new, and (3) not obvious. If your invention is a problem solver, chances are it's useful. A search of patents in existence will give you a good sense if it's new, or in Patent and Trademark Office terms, "novel." "Not obvious" is trickier. The rule is that if someone else in the field would naturally have stumbled upon your innovation, it's obvious and not patentable.

The reason I've emphasized that inventions are things, not ideas, is the fact that you can't patent an idea. Remember our example of Joe and Mary and the intermittent windshield wiper from Chapter 1? While you don't have to provide the USPTO with a working model, you do have to turn your idea into an invention ("reduce it to practice") and provide a detailed description of the invention sufficient to make the examiner believe your invention works. If Joe had told the USPTO that he had seen the need for an intermittent windshield wiper and wanted to protect his brilliant insight—claiming that no one else could create an intermittent wiper because it was his idea—they would have laughed at him. But Mary's case was different because she provided them with detailed drawings that showed precisely how her wiper invention actually worked. If he had done that before Mary, Joe would have gotten the patent.

Alas, Mary was disappointed in the end as well. Her licensing agreement with the automaker was for her patent on the "cam-driven device." One of the automaker's engineers took a look at her cam and said "I can improve this by using a purely electronic circuit." He designed one that had fewer parts, weighed less, had multiple speeds, and most importantly used no cams. The automaker got the patent on this. Because it was so much better they never used Mary's for anything. All she got from the deal was that small down payment which she had to use to pay for the divorce. *C'est la vie.*

Indignant, Mary sued the automaker for patent infringement. The court found in favor of the automaker, and justifiably so. Mary was in essence using the same argument that Joe had, saying "Hey! I came up with the idea of the intermittent wiper before the car maker did!" But as ex-husband Joe found out, you can't patent the idea of the intermittent wiper. You patent the machinery that makes a wiper operate intermittently. Her patent was for machinery that used cams. The automaker had a control unit that used an electronic circuit. The automaker's patent was for an improvement that was so novel that it was actually a different invention worthy of its own patent. Case closed.

I drew inspiration for the Joe and Mary story from an actual case in which Bob Kearns, inventor of an intermittent windshield wiper control unit back in the early 1960s, sued a number of American automotive companies for patent infringement.[5] This is a complex and controversial case, which I have changed and simplified to serve my need for a metaphor. In actuality, Mr. Kearns eventually prevailed, an outcome that is controversial to this day. As New Yorker author John Seabrook stated in a 1993 article about this case, "Patent law is maddeningly subjective and imprecise, and apt to plunge all but the stoutest minds into dizzying swirls of logic."[6] So don't use my stories as the basis for either a patent application or a lawsuit. Consult your patent attorney.

## DEFINING OUR TERMS

Patents, like trademarks, copyrights and trade secrets, are classes of intellectual property. But as we'll explore in Chapter 4, patents are essentially articles of personal property that can be sold outright or licensed in return for royalties, as I did with the needle protector.

## PATENT

A patent is a document issued by the federal government that grants the holder(s) the "right to exclude others from making, using or selling the invention throughout the United States or importing the invention into the United States" for a limited time, typically twenty years.[7] (Under special circumstances, patents on drugs, food additives and medical devices may be extended.[8]) Violating patent rights is known as infringement and can be litigated. (Patents can't be "renewed." After the term expires, others may copy your invention without infringing, but they cannot re-patent the invention.) There are three main types of patents: utility, design and plant.

> • The Patent and Trademark Office Website (www.uspto.gov) provides a comprehensive overview of patents, trademarks and copyrights, and includes detailed instructions on filing and registering.

**Utility Patent.** This is the most common type of patent. It applies to inventions that function in a unique manner and produce a useful result. In addition to being useful, new and nonobvious, an invention must fit into at least one of five statutory categories[9]:

1. *Compositions of matter—such as chemicals, drugs, plastics and fuels.*

2. *Manufactures or articles of manufacture—relatively simple (without working or moving parts as primary features) items that have been made by human hands or by machines; this can apply to everything from paper clips to buildings.*

3. *Machines or apparatuses—generally devices with moving parts that are used to perform a task, such as a cigarette lighter, wearable computer headset or gas engine.*

4. *Processes or methods—ways of doing or making things with one or more steps, such as pasteurization and software processes.*

5. *A new use or improvement of one of the above.*

Distinctions between these categories can be blurry, and while an examiner must conclude that your invention fits into one or more of them, you needn't state which one(s). Items that don't fall into one of these categories and thus don't qualify for utility patents include naturally occurring items, mental processes, natural laws and printed matter.

**Design Patent.** Good for fourteen years, these protect the unique, purely ornamental shape or design of a manufactured item (for example, Nike shoe designs).[10] The same item might have a utility patent covering its functional features and a design patent to protect its ornamental shape or design.

**Plant Patent.** These protect unique plant varieties that are produced through grafting or cuttings (asexually reproduced), such as hybrid tea roses or Better Boy tomatoes.[11]

## TRADEMARK (TM)

These are words, slogans, symbols, designs or some combination thereof that distinguish a product or service—the brand names that give products corporate identity, such as SKYY® Vodka, Coca-Cola's name and typeface, and the Nike swoosh. "Trademark" sometimes refers to a "service mark," which is the name by which a service, rather than a product, is promoted. McDonald's is a service mark (their service is selling food); Big Mac is a trademarked product.

## COPYRIGHT (©)

This protects published and unpublished literary, dramatic, musical and dance compositions, films, photographs, paintings, sculpture, other visual works of art, and computer programs from being copied. (For instance, the words on the SKYY® Vodka label are copyrighted.) Copyrights protect the expression of ideas, not the ideas themselves. In general, materials that were copyrighted in 1978 or later last the lifetime of the author, artist or designer plus seventy years.[12] Copyright protection begins automatically when the work is set on paper or otherwise fixed in tangible form. You can also obtain and fill out a form, send it back with the appropriate fee, and thus register your copyright, which can provide substantial benefits in the event of any conflicts or copyright infringement claims. Visit the United

States Copyright Office online at http://www.copyright.gov/.

## TRADE SECRET

This covers a wide spectrum of formulas, patterns, manufacturing processes, methods of doing business or technical know-how that give the holder competitive advantage and which are kept secret, such as the SKYY® Vodka distillation process or Coca-Cola's recipe. The Uniform Trade Secrets Act attempts to create uniform protection of trade secrets from state to state.[13] As of May 2013, 48 of the 50 United States had adopted the Uniform Trade Secrets Act[14] so if you intend to rely on trade secret protection you or your attorney need to know what that's all about.

## "PATENT PENDING"

This serves notice that you have sent a patent application to the USPTO. You can use the phrase only after the USPTO has received your application, otherwise you may be liable to the U.S. government for "false marking."

## BE THE FIRST TO FILE

It used to be that in the United States, patents were granted on a "first to invent" basis. That is, if you could prove that you had invented something before the other guy, you would be awarded the patent. Not anymore.

As of March 16, 2013,[15] patents are awarded on the "first to file" principle. Let's say that you and someone else file an application for what is essentially the same invention, but the USPTO receives your application a couple days earlier. Assuming there's no reason for the patent office to reject either application, your application will get preference because you were the first to file. It doesn't matter how long either of you have been working on your invention; it's all about whose application gets there first.

This was not always the case. When I wrote the first edition of this book, U.S. patent law followed a first-to-invent principle. Every other patent-issuing country in the world followed a first-to-file principle, which caused significant complication when a U.S. inventor wanted to patent abroad and play on the global field. In response to the economic turmoil and recession that began in 2008, significant pressure built up to bring the United States into alignment with the rest of the world and give parity to American companies. In 2011 Congress passed the Leahy-Smith America Invents Act ("AIA"), which among other things changed the American patent system from first-to-invent to first-to-file. There is a good deal of controversy over the change to first-to-file, with opponents saying it will stifle innovation and hurt the economy, and proponents saying it will stimulate innovation and help the economy. Time will tell.

One thing is certain: this poses a challenge for the small inventor. The little guy, working at home or with a small startup, might need years before being ready to file. A well-funded and established company may be able to do the same thing in weeks or months once they know what they are trying to accomplish. Under the old system, if the little guy could prove through witnesses and documentation that he or she had invented it first, he or she would tyoically get the patent. Now the advantage lies with the organization that has the resources or money to enable faster design and development. Not fair? Maybe not, but this has always been the case in regard to international patents. Nevertheless, the AIA includes provisions specifically intended to help the small inventor. For instance, the AIA establishes a "micro entity" category of applicants who are entitled to significantly lower USPTO fees. Among other things, such applicants have to certify that they qualify as a small entity, have not been named on four previously filed applications, and do not have a gross income exceeding three times the average gross income.[16] Additionally, Section 28 of the AIA requires the director of the USPTO to establish a Patent Ombudsman Program to provide "support and services relating to patent filings to small business concerns and independent inventors." In accordance with this provision, the USPTO established the Program for Small Business Concerns.[17] Section 28 of the AIA also provides that the Director shall work with intellectual property law associations to establish pro bono programs across the country to "assist financially under-resourced independent inventors and small businesses." There are other provisions that affect patent law and inventors, but the change to first-to-file is the most important.

## GET AN EXTRA YEAR: THE PROVISIONAL PATENT APPLICATION

You can lock in an earlier formal filing date by filing a provisional patent application. The date of the provisional filing becomes the patent's filing date of record, if you later file a full patent application.[18] It is important to realize that the provisional patent application does not convey any patent protection, but rather only provides a filing date. You must file a full patent application to obtain any patent protection for your invention.

You might consider a provisional application if you need to lock in a filing date, but you do not have the time or the money to prepare a full patent application. The provisional application is good for one year, and at some point prior to the end of the one year pendency period, you need to file a full patent application or lose the benefit of the earlier filing date of the provisional application.[19] Since the patent term is measured from the date the full patent application is filed, and not the date the provisional application is filed, a provisional patent application can extend the expiration date of the patent from twenty to twenty-one years of the provisional application. Filing a provisional application, however will likely delay the date on which the patent issues, so the actual enforceable term of the patent (measured from issuance to expiration) may not be significantly affected.

During this year under the provisional application you can finalize your product's design, post "patent pending" on your product, make sales, secure a licensee or prepare your formal patent application. Should your promotional results be disappointing, you needn't file a more expensive regular application, but keep in mind that you cannot legally post "patent pending" after the one-year provisional period expires if you have not filed a corresponding non-provisional application.

There are some potential pitfalls associated with filing a provisional application, and therefore great care must be taken in drafting a provisional application. Only those features that are fully disclosed in a provisional patent application are entitled to the earlier filing date. It can be difficult to know every feature that you will want to protect until you prepare a full patent application, complete with a full set of patent claims. Therefore, it is easy to disclose too little information in your provisional application. On the other hand, there are also dangers associated with disclosing too much information. If you disclose features of your product in your provisional application that are not later claimed in your full patent application, you may find yourself unable to obtain any protection for those unclaimed features at a later time. This is particularly dangerous if there are some unclaimed features of your product that could be protected as a trade secret. Therefore, if you file a provisional application, you should do your best to decide what features you will want to protect in your patent, and disclose only information that is relevant to those features in your patent application. Features that you do not want to patent – such as features that you want to keep as a trade secret – should not be disclosed in the provisional application. Because of these pitfalls, which can trip up even an experienced patent attorney, a provisional application should be considered a last resort to be used only if you absolutely must get a patent application on file to preserve the filing date. Otherwise, it is best to prepare and file a full patent application from the start.

A provisional application is faster, cheaper and simpler to file because it does not require formal language or draftsman-quality blueprints. You need not explain every detail of your product. A shorter description in plain English and informal drawings will suffice. But you will eventually need full documentation when you file a full patent application.

You need to consider very carefully whether you want a provisional patent application. The advantage, given the new first-to-file rule, is that even if your product is not quite ready for prime time, you can file anyway and hopefully get a jump on the competition. The disadvantage is that the moment you file the clock starts ticking and you'd better be ready with your full application before the year expires. Some people choose to file provisional applications late in the development process so they can include the most accurate and broad terminology in their patent. Your provisional and regular (non-provisional) applications should not contain significant differences, which is another argument for filing the provisional application late in your development process. But if you delay too long you may lose out to a faster competitor.

## THE GRACE PERIOD

Generally speaking, an item that is publicly known is not patentable because it is "prior art." So you'd best keep your inventions to yourself until you have patent protection. However, in some circumstances your invention might be discussed or disclosed publicly, either intentionally or unintentionally, before you are ready to patent. In this case, U.S. patent law allows a one-year grace period in which you can speak publicly about your idea and still receive a patent. In this regard, the U.S. system is different from true first-to-file systems found in most countries. In such countries, a public disclosure prior to filing a patent application acts as an absolute bar.

Let's suppose you and a colleague have been working on a new invention for years. He's a blabbermouth and tells an industry journalist who then publishes an article about it on February 1, 2013. At that moment of initial public disclosure the clock starts ticking and you have until February 1, 2014 to file your patent in the U.S. due to the grace period. If you let it go past that date your patent claim is most likely to be rejected as being prior art.

Thus, it is not just what you as an inventor may do that could comprise of a public disclosure. Public use, sales, and other disclosures by third parties (both within the United States and in foreign countries[20]) may also start the clock running. Alternatively, let's say you publicly disclose your invention, and then another inventor tries to file after your disclosure but before you have filed your application. So long as you file within the one-year grace period, you would be entitled to the patent even though the other guy filed before you. So the timing and nature of your disclosures requires some strategy. By disclosing, you could block better-funded competitors from receiving patents, but that same disclosure will likely cause your foreign patent rights to be forfeited. You also run the significant risk of forfeiting your U.S. patent rights if your application is not timely filed after that disclosure. These are some of the many complexities you should discuss with a patent attorney or other expert.

> • Inventor's Journals, logbooks with complete instructions for inventors, are available from the Inventions, Patents and Trademarks Company; The Inventor's Notebook, available from Nolo Press, includes worksheets, checklists, and sample agreements. See appendix for contact information.

## DOCUMENTING THINGS "JUST IN CASE"

I used to advise inventors to document everything, from sudden brainstorms to developmental sketches to detailed functional descriptions. This was because of the now discarded first-to-invent rule. You had to be able to prove that you had invented something first if you were to defeat a competitor's application. This is now virtually useless for the purposes of obtaining a patent.

I believe you should still document things in this way, but for different reasons. Suppose you invent something and you are working on your patent application. Then a big rich company develops essentially the same product and gets a patent because they filed before you. Perhaps they got wind of your idea and were able to act quicker than you. Maybe they came up with it all on their own. If you have properly documented everything it is possible that you might have grounds to bring suit against them. This is good news because one cannot simply copy another's invention and be entitled to a patent by virtue of being the first to file an application. The AIA provides for "derivation proceedings" to allow the USPTO to police such activities.[21] If your case has any merit at all the folks who patented it could choose to settle out of court and pay you just to make you go away.

For this, you will need clear documentation of your invention, including descriptions and sketches. Use a bound book (something that makes the deceptive insertion of pages less likely) with numbered pages (or number them yourself). Check stationery or office supply stores for lab, engineering or accounting notebooks. Write in ink and don't tear out pages, black anything out, or leave large blank spaces. Every time you have an idea that you think has any value, make a note of it, or draw a picture of it.

You can write up an invention disclosure document to help prove its date of conception. Briefly summarize your invention with a descriptive title (not necessarily its ultimate trademark), the background of the invention (that is, products that are currently in use), a short description of the invention itself, sketches, a detailed rundown of how the invention works, and a list of its unique features. Include your name, address and telephone number, and then date and sign it. Have two uninterested, unrelated witnesses sign and date it, stating that they understand the invention. Have the disclosure notarized or send it to your patent attorney. Make sure you keep it confidential so it does not end up counting as a public disclosure that would trigger the one-year grace period. It is the signatures and dates by those other witnesses that will establish when you had your brainstorm—the "date of original conception"— and how you have reduced it to practice. Just remember that an invention disclosure is not a substitute for continuing to maintain full and accurate logs of your inventing process. Note that the USPTO used to offer a Disclosure Document Program but that has been discontinued.

## NONDISCLOSURE AGREEMENTS

When you show someone your idea before its launch or patenting, consider using confidentiality or nondisclosure agreements, particularly to ensure that the public use, sale, or disclosure bar is not triggered. (See the sample agreement in the appendix. They can also be obtained in legal form books or from your attorney.) They are a simple, important part of your paper trail and don't imply paranoia on your part or distrust of the "disclosee." They can be used when you show your developing product to people you hire to help you at various steps, to potential licensees or manufacturing partners, and even to people you ask to sign and witness your invention disclosure. Remember to give the disclosee a completed copy of the document. You can also ask disclosees to sign and date your inventor's logbook or journal under a legend stating that they have seen and understood your confidential invention, as described on such and such notebook page(s).

I am currently developing a pillow filled with microfiber that won't stay crushed down or become misshapen. When I go to a manufacturer to help me create samples, I share my design and contact information for other suppliers. I use a nondisclosure to prevent this manufacturer from using or talking about my design.

> • A "poor man's patent search" consists of checking to see if your product is already on sale in stores, online, through catalogs or at trade shows.

If someone balks at signing a nondisclosure, you have to weigh the situation and decide whether to trust the person. It used to be that you had first-to-invent rules in your favor, but from now onwards you have to be the first to file. My cautious recommendation is to forget about anyone who does not want to sign a nondisclosure and find someone who will. If you really want what they have to offer, you might have to take a deep breath and go for it. Your recourse, if someone has signed a nondisclosure and then breached it, is suing, which is costly and time-consuming. So strive to work with trustworthy people in any event.

## CONDUCTING A PATENT SEARCH

Whether or not you decide to apply for a patent for your invention, doing a patent search early on in your creative process is important if only to make sure you aren't infringing on someone else's patent and opening yourself up to a lawsuit. But most of the time, you want to find out if your invention is patentable or not; if you discover it's not, you thus save yourself a great deal of development time and the cost of a patent application. You can do this initial search yourself or hire patent searchers, a patent agent, or a patent attorney to do it for you. I recommend that you first conduct a search on your own for several reasons: doing a search can educate you about how to write your own application, about "prior art" components and technologies and about what has succeeded or failed in the past. It's also cheaper.

However, I also recommend that once you have conducted a preliminary search on your own and found no impediments, you should contact a patent attorney (or other professional) to conduct a more thorough—and costly—search. While I don't believe in wasting money, I also don't believe in cutting corners. If Al and I turn up a patent roadblock on our own, we save ourselves the money and don't bother contacting our attorney, but we also know better than to get deep into product development without having an expert do a comprehensive patent search. Cutting corners here has a way of backfiring. How would you like to conduct or pay for an incomplete, bargain-priced patent search, then spend thousands of dollars prototyping and maybe even pitching your invention, and then find you are infringing on an existing patent? Don't let that happen. Your preliminary patent search is only a yellow light; proceed with caution until a patent attorney tells you the way is clear, then go for it. (We'll talk more about the pros and cons of hiring patent attorneys below.)

One way to start your patent search is by going to one of the Patent and Trademark Resource Centers (formerly called Patent and Trademark Depository Libraries). These contain copies of patent office records and often hold periodic classes on how to do your own search. They are located at selected public libraries, state libraries, and university libraries across the U.S. For the one nearest you, visit http://www.uspto.gov/products/library/index.jsp or call 800-PTO-9199.

Internet searches, that rely entirely on searching key words, may be less effective then searches that also rely on patent classification—a prior patent much like yours may simply use different descriptive terms. Using the USPTO online search engine to perform both a keyword search and a classification search is a thorough approach for uncovering relevant prior art. Another option, if you are inclined to make a trek to Arlington, Virginia, is to perform a search at the USPTO of the repository of patents and prior art references that is used by the USPTO patent examiners. This approach can be helpful since the USPTO repository includes not only US patents and patent applications, but also foreign patents and a limited amount of non-patent prior art, such as product advertising materials. Keep in mind, however, that there are some drawbacks performing your search at the USPTO. Patents are organized at the USPTO based upon their classification, and in some instances patents may be misclassified. You're not likely to find a misclassified patent when searching at the USPTO, whereas an online keyword search might uncover the reference. Furthermore, examiners at the USPTO sometime take prior art references that are relevant to their work from the repositories to their offices until they are finished with them. If the patent examiner has temporarily removed a reference from the USPTO repository, you will not uncover that reference during a search at the USPTO.

> • The rights granted by a U.S. patent have no effect in foreign countries. If you want patent protection in other countries, you must apply in those other countries. Remember that taking advantage of the "grace period" permitted under U.S. law typically will prohibit you from obtaining patent rights in foreign countries that don't have such a grace period. Since the laws of other countries vary, working with a patent attorney skilled in obtaining foreign patents is advised.

The USPTO patent search engine provides full-text searches of US patents issued since 1976, as well as published US patent applications. Other patent-related sites that offer texts of patents include Google Patents (www.google.com/patents), FreePatentsOnline.com (www. freepatentsonline.com) and Micropatent (www.micropatent.com). Some of these websites offer full-text searches of US patents over a greater period of time compared to that of the USPTO website, as well as searches of some international patents and published patent applications, such as EPO and WIPO published patent applications. They also allow you to download PDF copies of patents. A good website for searching international patents and published patent applications is maintained by the World Intellectual Property Organization, or "WIPO" (http://patentscope.wipo.int/search/en/search.jsf). This resource allows you to search patents from a number of countries and regional patent offices in Europe, Asia, Africa and the Middle East. The European patent office, or "EPO", also provides a number of tools on its website for searching EPO published patent applications (http://www.epo.org/searching/free/espacenet.html). Additionally, Japanese patents can also be searched at the Industrial Property Digital Library (http://www.ipdl.inpit.go.jp/homepg_e.ipdl).

Advanced patent search engines are available through Westlaw IP and LEXIS-NEXIS TotalPatent. These websites offer full-text searches of foreign patents (such as European and Asian patents) in addition to US patents, and they provide a variety of powerful search tools and other features that are not available elsewhere. These services are provided on a subscription basis, are extremely expensive, and are relatively complex to use compared to other free resources available online. Some public law libraries, however, may have subscriptions to one or both of these legals research websites. Therefore, you may have unlimited free access to these services at your local law library. There may even be staff members at the library who can provide advice on how to perform patent searches on these websites. Check with your local law library to see what online patent search resources are available.

How do you conduct a patent search for an invention that is so unique you have no idea what others might have called it? You need a United States Patent Classification number (USPC). You can search the USPTO's Office of Patent Classification online (http://www.uspto.gov/patents/resources/classification/index.jsp) to discover the number appropriate for your invention, and then use that number to identify other inventions in the same category. The U.S. and Europe began harmonizing their classification number systems in 2010 under the Cooperative Patent Classification system (CPC), to "migrate towards a common classification scheme".[22] This is good news, since the use of one system will make it easier and faster to get accurate international patent search results.

Or you can write or fax the USPTO, describing your idea, how it works and so on, and including a rough sketch. They'll get back to you in a few weeks with a classification number. Write to USPTO, Public Search Facility, Madison East, First Floor, 600 Dulany Street, Alexandria VA, 22314.

When and if you decide to hire professional help, you can find patent searchers, patent agents and patent attorneys online or in the Yellow Pages. In addition, the U.S. Patent and Trademark Office reference, a page-turner available in most library reference departments, lists agents and attorneys in Attorneys and Agents Registered to Practice.

## APPLYING FOR A PATENT

Step-by-step instructions for filling out a patent application can be obtained from the USPTO (or on their website). In simplest terms, applying for a patent goes like this: You (or you and your attorney) prepare an application and send it to the USPTO. At the USPTO, a patent examiner reviews it. More often than not, you will be asked to respond to objections and make changes, additions or deletions. If the application is rejected outright, you have the right to try and convince the examiner that he or she is in error. If your application is ultimately allowed, you pay the issue fee and publication fee, and then the USPTO grants your patent. The whole process generally takes one to three years.

As with everything else these days, patent filing has gone electronic. The USPTO now encourages applicants to use EFS-Web, their web-based patent application and document submission solution to file patents[23]. You can still file using paper forms and documentation and send them via snail mail, but there is now a $400 surcharge for doing so. Filing online is also likely to be faster, potentially gaining you a slightly earlier filing date. See http://www.uspto.gov/patents/process/file/efs/index.jsp for more information.

Your application consists of a transmittal letter, drawings of the invention, the "claims" you are making about your invention, an "abstract" summary, the Patent Application Declaration Form and the "specification" which describes the invention. There are several parts to the specification, ranging from the title of the invention and its background in terms of prior art to a description of its operation and a discussion of alternative embodiments. (See why I have a patent attorney? Just thinking about this makes me want a Blue Angel martini.)

At this point, you might be wondering: Why bother with all of this? Simply put, patent protection preserves your right to make money with your innovations. It's hard to command a price from a licensee without a patent, and having a patent can sometimes help you to raise money. Also, having a patent can slow down your competitors, who may have to redesign their similar product in order to avoid infringing on your patent. However, while it's true that inventors in the United States enjoy a very high level of patent protection, and the courts usually find in favor of patent holders in patent infringement cases, some people don't believe the benefits outweigh the costs. Patents are expensive to apply for in the first place, and keep in mind that patent rights are not self-enforcing. That means that if someone violates your patent, the USPTO won't do anything to defend it on your behalf; you will need to defend it yourself. That can be very costly and time consuming. It's worth reiterating that having a patent is no guarantee that you'll be able to manufacture, sell or license your invention. Many, many existing patents are not protecting existing products. Maybe the patent holder discovered there was no market for the invention or perhaps a better product was produced and patented in the same field before he or she could get to market. Some people get patents simply so that they can frame them and hang them on their walls. This is silly.

Let me also reiterate that protecting your idea isn't the same thing as evaluating your idea's viability in the marketplace. You must do both if you are serious about marketing your innovations. Assessing and ensuring your ability to get a patent is part of exploring the viability of your invention.

> • Periodic maintenance fees must be paid to the USPTO in order to keep an issued patent in effect.

It is also important to remember that obtaining a patent on your invention does not give you the right to "practice" that invention, only the right to exclude others from making, using or selling it. The USPTO has no jurisdiction over questions relating to infringement of patents. In examining applications for patents, they make no determination as to whether the invention infringes any prior patent. An improvement invention may be patentable, but still might infringe a prior unexpired patent for the invention improved upon. Even though you have an issued patent, your invention may still infringe someone else's patent.

Deciding when to apply for a patent depends partly on the specifics of your invention and your plans for manufacturing or licensing. Here are some things to consider:

- *Applying before you assess the needs of the marketplace and before researching existing patents is never advisable.*

- *It's ideal to have a patent or patent pending status before approaching a potential licensee.*

- *Getting a patent before you build a prototype can be risky. You may find you need to modify your plans significantly enough in your prototyping process to make the patent protection you've applied for inadequate.*

- *If you know your invention is a fad or fashion sensitive item that will realistically be marketed for a limited amount of time, or if your estimated profits will be fairly small, you should consider skipping the time and expense of patenting. Unpatented or unpatentable ideas can still produce profit.*

> • Inventor's groups, such as the United Inventors Association of the USA (http://www.uiausa.org/), may provide tips on good patent attorneys near you.

An argument in favor of patents is that they protect you when you pitch your invention to potential licensees or manufacturers. (We'll talk more about this in the next chapter.) Idea theft is not as rampant as the news media would have us believe, but it does happen, so don't risk it. If you don't want to wait until you have full patent protection, which as we've seen can be costly and time-consuming, "patent pending" status can deter thieves. You can claim patent pending status after filing either a provisional or a permanent (non-provisional) patent application. If you file neither of these, use a nondisclosure agreement. Legally, once you've told someone your trade secret, you can no longer claim exclusive rights to it.

## INVENTORS ASSISTANCE CENTER (IAC)

You should also know about the Inventors Assistance Center (IAC), an office set up specifically to help you navigate the USPTO system. They can provide a lot of help but keep in mind that they cannot answer questions concerning a particular patent application, give you an opinion as to whether an invention is patentable, or provide legal advice.[24] Visit them at http://www.uspto.gov/inventors/iac/index.jsp

> • If a patent attorney is convinced your invention will be a moneymaker, he or she may agree to provide services against future revenues.

## GUERILLA TACTICS: GO TO MARKET BEFORE PATENTING

One patenting strategy is to put your product on the market before filing a US patent application. This way, you can spend your money on marketing rather than on filing patents, and hopefully generate some income before incurring the expense of a patent. If you find your product is a dud, you can skip patenting altogether. There are risks with this approach. You can file for a patent up to one year after you first sell or otherwise disclose your invention (see "The Grace Period" earlier in this chapter) but by taking advantage of this delay you run the risk of someone else filing first. While the sales of your product might prevent the other parties earlier-filed application from being used as prior art against you under an exception to the new first-to-file rules, there may be situations where that is not the case. In particular, if the disclosure of the other party's patent application is in some ways different from your product, but is still covered by your patent claims, then the other patent application might constitute prior art against your patent claims despite your prior sales. It is still uncertain of how the USPTO and the courts will interpret these aspects of the new patent laws. Because of this uncertainty, you should be careful about making any public disclosure of your invention before filing a patent application.

Additionally, while the US offers a one-year grace period, the vast majority of foreign countries do not offer any grace period. Therefore, if you make any public disclosure of your invention before filing your US patent application, you will lose the ability to file a patent application in most foreign countries. If you're contemplating seeking foreign patent protection, do not make any public disclosure of your invention before filing your US patent application.

## APPLYING EVEN IF A PATENT IS UNLIKELY

I've never done this, but another strategy is to apply for a patent yourself (and save the attorney fees) when you know your product will not be eligible for significant protection. By applying yourself, you still enter the "patent pending" phase, you may delay competition, and you may improve your chances with investors and licensees. You can let your application expire if you decide not to proceed before the patent is issued.

## STICK SOME IMPROVEMENTS ON IT

Zip Notes™ is my patented battery-powered sticky note dispenser. The first version we patented used a small rubber belt to grab a roll of paper and feed it out. After a couple years I came up with the idea of using a gear motor with a polished plastic drum to engage the stickum. This works far better, is cheaper to produce, is smaller, and can't break. We patented this and began phasing out the belted version. This improvement effectively extended our patent protection to twenty four years: three years for the belt version, plus one year of protection under a preliminary patent application for the drum version, plus twenty years of formal patent protection for the drum version. Of course someone could have looked at the belt version and patented their own drum version if they were smarter and faster than I am, but most copycats aren't that creative. They think in terms of copying, not inventing. When the first patent for the belt version expires, anyone is free to copy and produce it. But that is the more complex, larger, more expensive, less competitive version, so why would they? And maybe in the next year or two I'll come up with yet another patentable improvement that will extend my effective protection still further. I'll talk more about Zip Notes™ in Chapter 4.

## DON'T DELAY

Under the new "First to File" rules, a delay in filing opens you to the risk that a competitor might file before you, and snatch that patent right out from under you. Some advanced players may still try to gain an advantage by intentionally lining up improved versions and patenting them every couple years (similar to what I did with Zip Notes™), but this is risky and I don't recommend it. If you have an improvement, patent it and start producing.

If you're beginning to feel that figuring out when, how and why to apply for a patent is too complicated to decide on your own, keep reading.

## HIRING A PATENT ATTORNEY

You don't need to employ a patent attorney in order to obtain a patent. But there are several good reasons to consider hiring one, not the least of which is that he or she can help you develop the best strategy for your situation. In my opinion, you should only write your own patent application if, first, you are already a talented writer, and second, you are motivated to take time away from inventing to learn the ropes of the process. A good patent attorney, on the other hand, can

1. *Probably write a better application than you*

2. *Do a more thorough patent search than you*

3. *Save you time, and ultimately*

4. *Save you money*

My patent attorney and good friend for more than thirty-five years was Mike Ebert. He was a wonderful man with an extraordinary ability to draft strong patents. When he was a young attorney just starting out, the higher-ups at his firm handed him a task they didn't want—writing a patent for a newfangled copier. This Xerox patent is now featured in law textbooks as a model of solid patent writingMike's work was so good that Xerox tried, and failed, to talk him into going to work for them. Their loss was my gain.

When Mike retired, I tried to replace him and that was daunting. Sadly, he died a few years ago and I miss him a lot. Our long relationship casts some light on what to seek in a patent attorney. Most fundamentally, you need to be able to communicate well with him or her. I could call Mike on the phone, describe my idea and detail its mechanics, and Mike would "get it" instantly and start writing it up. If an attorney has an inaccurate understanding of your invention, or if he or she doesn't quickly get your drift, go elsewhere.

Some people advise shopping for a patent attorney who has experience as a litigator. Their reasoning is that these attorneys may be more careful about avoiding loopholes in their patent writing. You might also consider looking for a patent attorney who has written patents for other inventions in your technical field, or seek out someone who has an educational background in your invention area. You may be able to find a good one through referrals and networking. A quick and highly unscientific search for legal services on the LinkedIn website using the keyword "patent" delivered tens of thousands of results.

Once you've finished your own preliminary patent search, and you're interviewing potential patent attorneys to write the actual application, here are some smart questions to ask:

- *Is my product eligible for a broad claim?*

- *Will I be able to obtain a single-feature claim?*

- *To what degree will a competitor have to change my product to avoid my patent?*

- *Which of my product features will a patent protect?*

- *Do any of the patents I've uncovered prevent me from selling my product?*

- *If I do get a patent, are you (the attorney) willing to take a patent infringement case on a contingency basis? (They can be extremely costly.)*

· *What parts of the product can't be changed without losing protection,*
*once I've applied for the patent?*[25]

While you must be able to trust your patent attorney and the other experts you work with, you can't turn off your own brain. Educate yourself so that you can make informed decisions with your expert advisors. Trust your gut and be willing to take calculated risks, not because you're a daredevil who's hell-bent on ignoring all received wisdom, but because you have done your homework and have the courage of your convictions. As James Gleick once wrote in the *New York Times Magazine*, inventors are "a familiar species of fraud victim. An entire industry of invention promoters promises to help inventors get patents, usually charging thousands of dollars in fees that are virtually never recouped." (Gleick, March 12, 2000)

You avoid becoming a fraud victim by becoming savvy. My D-Fuzz-It® patent attorney cautioned me, warning that getting a patent wouldn't guarantee me a damn thing. I took his real-world warnings to heart and forged ahead anyway, certain that I could market the device. I'm glad I did. Conversely, when my friend Knud Dyby was advised by a model maker not to seek a patent for his ingenious paper clip holder/dispenser, he should have gotten a second opinion from a good patent attorney. We seek advisors who are knowledgeable and trustworthy. Cultivate those qualities in yourself so that you can exercise good judgment about taking and overriding any advice you receive.

A patent attorney can obtain a thorough patent search and then assess its results for you. Unlike your preliminary search, this will include a complete domestic and worldwide search conducted at the Patent and Trademark Office by an experienced searcher who uses both manual and computer search techniques. This person will confirm with a patent examiner that the search is conducted in the proper fields. The patent attorney will then review the search and give a legal opinion on your potential patent's commercial value. This is another reason to be wary of inventor service organizations, which benefit by telling you that you have a great idea and should file immediately. They'll get more money out of you that way, whether it's true or not. Use an attorney you trust instead.

A patent attorney can save you time because, as you've probably gathered, assembling a solid patent application is time consuming. (Wouldn't you rather be inventing?) What's more, it takes skill. There are solid patents with "teeth" and "loose" patents that don't provide much protection.

The claims are the most important part of the application. They determine the scope of your patent rights. A skilled attorney will write your claims in a way that makes them unassailable. A strong patent is one that makes a straightforward, simple claim with one or two key words or phrases. The more key words or phrases, the weaker the patent, since another invention has to infringe on them all to warrant your protest. Patents with broad claims are strong because a wide variety of specific designs may infringe on that patent.

I couldn't have patented the entire "needle protector" concept, just my particular needle protector. But I could describe my needle and make claims about it that ward off infringement. For instance, if I had defined a particular material as being integral to my device, another inventor who used a different material could say her device is different. In our first claim for the needle protector, we describe "a push rod of flexible material slidable on the track and terminating at its lower end on a finger rest which when engaged by a finger of an operator advanced the rod from a retracted to an extended position." The operation is described with no limiting details. The finger rest shape is not detailed and the "flexible material" is not defined.

Finally, despite their up-front cost, patent attorneys can ultimately save you money because missed deadlines and other filing errors can cost hundreds of dollars in extra fees. Plus, getting the fullest patent protection possible could well save you money in the long run by protecting you against infringement litigation.

## (ENDNOTES)

1 http://www.cdc.gov/niosh/stopsticks/

2 35 U.S.C. 154 This is a reference to the federal law code of the United States, meaning "Title 35 of the United States Code, section 154. There will be many similar references structured like this in this book, and future references will consist only of the alphanumeric code.

3 http://www.uspto.gov/web/offices/ac/ido/oeip/taf/us_stat.htm

4 http://www.wipo.int/export/sites/www/freepublications/en/statistics/943/wipo_pub_943_2012.pdf

5 http://www.newyorker.com/archive/1993/01/11/1993_01_11_038_TNY_CARDS_000363341

6 http://www.newyorker.com/archive/1993/01/11/1993_01_11_038_TNY_CARDS_000363341

7 35 U.S.C. 154(a)(1)-(2)

8 35 U.S.C. 156

9 35 U.S.C. 101

10 35 U.S.C. 171-173

11 35 U.S.C. 161-164

12 17 U.S.C. 302

13 http://www.uniformlaws.org/shared/docs/trade%20secrets/utsa_final_85.pdf

14 http://www.lexology.com/library/detail.aspx?g=36d9a72c-9cdb-42bc-bab8-f5446ccfb5d8

15 America Invents Act, Section 3(n)(1). A simpler explanation can be found at the USPTO website FAQ: http://www.uspto.gov/aia_implementation/faqs_first_inventor.jsp

16 P.L. 112-29 at section 10(g) Full text available at http://www.uspto.gov/aia_implementation/20110916-pub-l112-29.pdf

17 http://www.uspto.gov/blog/aia/entry/uspto_establishes_patent_ombudsman_program

18 35 U.S.C. 111(b) See also Nolo's Guide to Provisional Patent Applications, © 2013 by Nolo Press. Available online at http://nolonow.nolo.com/noe/popup/provisional_patent_application_guide.pdf

19 35 U.S.C. 111(b) and 119(e)

20 35 U.S.C. 102(b)

21 P.L. 112-29 Section 3(h)

22 http://www.uspto.gov/patents/resources/classification/index.jsp

23 http://www.uspto.gov/patents/process/file/efs/index.jsp

24 http://www.uspto.gov/inventors/iac/index.jsp

25 Entrepreneur Magazine: Bringing Your Product to Market, Don Debelak. Copyright © 1997 by Don Debelak. Reprinted by permission of John Wiley & Sons, Inc.

# 4.

# Manufacture or License?
## Rolling Out Zip Notes

Little pads of sticky notes have been an office essential for a few decades now. You know them best by 3M's Post-it® trademark. They are mighty handy, but I often need to write more than what will fit on a three-by-three note and I end up with little trains of yellow squares all over my business documents. If one gets pulled off or is out of order the whole message gets screwed up. Also, I am forever pulling two or more off the pad at a time, which is a waste. And the pads are always walking off, seemingly of their own volition but more often in my pocket (where I can't find them) or in someone else's.

In my usual way, I got to thinking how I could make a common and highly useful product even more useful. My three pet peeves all centered on the most basic element of this ingenious invention: you're limited to the size and shape of the pad.

Paper is manufactured in rolls. Why not get a roll of three-inch-wide paper, put the low-tack adhesive on the back, and just tear off as much or as little as is needed? The adhesive would go in a strip down the middle to help prevent the paper from curling up. I would manufacture small, simple machines that would dispense as much or as little paper as was needed at the moment. I even had a great name: Rollit®. Ta-Da!

What about the adhesive? I had noticed that on some envelopes the post office applies a removable paper strip with a barcode. Those strips use an adhesive that can be repositioned and was exactly like what I needed. I did a little research and found the firm that applied the adhesive. The manager assured me it would be very easy to put the same stuff right down the center of a long roll of paper. I had found my source of "pre-gummed" paper.

Now on to the dispenser. I envisioned a little machine that rolled out the paper at the touch of a button. There would be a small serrated metal blade mounted to the housing so you could tear off the length you need, like a tape dispenser.

Al Kolvites and I sketched out a neat little mechanism that used a low-speed three-volt gear motor to drive a rubber belt. The belt turned an axle that had a rubber wheel on its other end. You press a button on the top and as the motor turns, both the belt and wheel press gently against the paper and push it out a slot in the machine's housing. The paper keeps coming out as long as you hold down the button. The whole thing was a little smaller than a desktop electric pencil sharpener and ran on two AA batteries.

Our Rollit® prototype was pretty rough looking. We repositioned the motor a few times, changed the tension on the belt, and made other adjustments. We cleaned it up, Al made our formal drawings, and my patent attorney Mike Ebert wrote up the patent application. We got a patent on the Rollit® machine with little hassle. We did not try to patent the paper with the adhesive down the middle because I did not believe I could patent the location of a stripe of glue.

Al then went about building the models from which our molds would be made. This was in the days before 3D printers so he used the standard machining techniques of the time. At this stage, everything has to be exactly right—or as right as possible—to avoid having to pay for expensive alterations to the mold later on. And there are almost always alterations to the mold. Early on we had identified the exact gear motor we wanted. We got assurances from the motor supplier that it would be in production for some time so we made arrangements to purchase tens of thousands. We designed the Rollit® innards to fit that gear motor. We made similar arrangements for the rubber belt and tire. It can be very costly if one of your suppliers unexpectedly discontinues or significantly alters a component you rely upon. You'll either have to redesign parts of your machine or pay a different supplier to begin manufacturing an equivalent component. So do your homework in advance and make sure your outsourced parts will be available.

I had considered licensing Rollit®—allowing someone else to produce and market it in return for payments to me—but in the end decided to manufacture it. I had experience manufacturing many products by now, and was comfortable with the process. I had also suspected—rightly or wrongly—that it would be easier and more profitable to manage manufacturing of this very promising product than to work with any of the big corporations that might have an interest in licensing it.

I already had an overseas manufacturing firm in mind and we worked out an agreement. This would be a one-stop shop for me since they could do the molding, order the motor and belts, assemble everything, pack it, and ship it out. Our agreement also covered them installing two AA batteries in each unit, because I intended to add consumer value by including the batteries.

I had some very specific batteries in mind. The ones I like are made in China on equipment produced in South Korea. Their lifespan is about 3% shorter but they are very high quality, they don't leak, and they cost about 20% less than the leading brands found in American stores. So the overall value is better. I made arrangements for my manufacturer to order the batteries they'd need.

We made about 50,000 of the original belt-drive Rollit®, and went to market in about 2006. We sold a bunch and people seemed to like them. We also came out with a manual version that functions like a tape dispenser: you pull the notepaper out by hand and tear it off. Things looked good. Then we encountered two big problems, and later a third.

First, we got a very stern letter from 3M corporation almost as soon as we went to market. They claimed that my name Rollit® infringed upon their Post-it® trademark and they were suing me. They also did not like my tagline, "Don't post it, Roll It!" I argued to the judge that the only similarity in the name was the word "it," and that because I had created the D-Fuzz-It® Sweater Comb about forty years earlier, 3M was potentially infringing upon my trademark. It was a nice try but 3M prevailed. So now I had the wrong name molded into about fifty thousand Rollits® and printed on the boxes. Fortunately, part of this agreement was that I could sell out my existing inventory and 3M paid me a reasonable sum to carry me through the re-naming. This was very helpful because I would have to change the molds and redesign all my packaging and support material. Fortunately, I had the name Zip Notes™ already lined up, and we've been using that ever since.

The second problem was that the batteries started leaking. There were my thousands of now-surplus Rollits®, sitting in warehouses, with their batteries beginning to ooze nasty fluids and mess things up. Livid, I took some of the failed batteries to the battery supplier. "What's wrong with your batteries? They're ruining my product!" They took the batteries away and said they'd look into it. I soon had their answer: Those were not their batteries, and they proved it to my satisfaction. Someone had illegally duplicated their label and put it on a far inferior grade of battery, and those were installed in my machines.

Using more of my frequent flier miles, I raced to the other side of the continent and confronted the manufacturer. "What's with these batteries? You've ripped me off and wrecked my machines!" They smiled and apologized most profusely, saying they had fired the man responsible as soon as they had found out. *Bah!* Needless to say that was the end of that relationship. Those idiots had cost me a ton of money, thrown away a lucrative client, violated trademark and copyright law, and destroyed any possibility of a future relationship with the real battery manufacturer—all so they could make a few illegitimate cents on each battery they installed. I retrieved my molds, found a new manufacturer, and paid them to replace the Rollit® mark on the molds with the Zip Notes™ mark.

I still had almost 50,000 Rollits® in their boxes, in their shipping cartons, stacked in a warehouse, each with potentially leaky batteries. I worked out a deal to buy the correct batteries in neat little cellophane two-packs. We opened up every Rollit® that went out our door, removed the batteries, placed a two-pack of new batteries in the box, and then re-packed everything. If the old batteries had been leaking, we set that unit aside for cleaning and separate sale. Some of the newer Zip Notes™ branded units had also received the bad batteries and got the same treatment. All this devoured our profit, but what was the alternative? Better to sell them all and recover some of our costs than to not sell any.

Throughout all this the belt-drive system continued to work splendidly. But I was never fully happy with it. I always thought the rubber belt might eventually break or start slipping. I was unhappy with the number of parts it required and the amount of space they took up. My inventor's mindset kept me wondering how I could improve it, to reduce the size of the unit, ensure longevity, and cut the number of parts. Remember that the more parts, the more likely it is to break down and the greater your cost of production.

When I used my manual version, my finger often got stuck to the adhesive and I would pull out more than expected. What if I were to use that to my advantage?

I started experimenting with this line of thinking. I installed a smooth plastic drum on the output shaft of the gear motor and laid the adhesive strip across it. When the motor turned on, the stickum stuck to the drum. By getting the geometry of the housing just right, I could apply enough gentle pressure over the adhesive to keep it engaged with the drum, and it peeled right off as it exited through the output slot. In effect, the paper had become its own conveyor belt.

Model One—the belt version—had just become obsolete but I was fine with that. Considering all the changes at Rollit®—whoops, I mean

Zip Notes™—retooling seemed a sensible thing now. We patented the new drum mechanism (which had the added benefit of extending our total patent protection, as I explained in Chapter 3) and went into production. Model Two—the drum version—was far better, being simpler, smaller, and cheaper to produce. I still include the batteries, but they are the right ones and are wrapped separately.

I made 100,000 of Model Two, all in navy blue. This was a management mistake. Based on the enthusiastic early reception of Rollit® I thought we would sell out of Zip Notes™ very quickly and that one color would be fine. But sales have been slower, because not everyone wants navy blue and because we had lost our management and sales momentum throughout all these legal and manufacturing gyrations.

Model Three is in development, which uses Model Two's drum mechanism in a smaller housing so it takes up less space. This time we will mold it in a variety of colors, including transparent so you can see how much paper is left and watch the mechanism work. As before, batteries will be included but wrapped separately. And you can bet I'll watch the manufacturer like a hawk.

The situation with the manufacturer was a major part of the Zip Notes™ story. So let's take a look at one of your most important management decisions: When to manufacture your new product yourself as we did, and when to license it to someone else.

## MAKING IT: WHEN TO MANUFACTURE

You've diligently perfected your invention, and perhaps applied for a patent. Now what? Most inventors, including this one, would be ready to make some money. Even if you have decided not to pursue a patent, you have something to make or sell.

In and of themselves, inventions and patents don't produce income. You make money with your patent and/or product by manufacturing or licensing. Actually, it may be more accurate to say that your decision is whether to go into business yourself or to form an alliance with another entity. There are many options within each choice.

> *The key to success isn't much good until one discovers the right lock to insert it in.*
>
> **TEHYI HSIEH,** *CHINESE EPIGRAMS INSIDE OUT*

If you go into business yourself, you might undertake everything—manufacturing, distribution and sales—or you might contract out one or more of these tasks. Indeed, I don't own or operate any manufacturing plants; I contract with various manufacturers to produce my products to my specifications, and after the Rollit® adventure you can bet I watch those specifications pretty closely.

If you don't launch your own product-based business, you may sell the rights to your product outright or license them to some degree to a third party. By entering into a licensing agreement, you (the licensor) grant a company or individual (the licensee) the rights a patent gives you—to manufacture, sell and use your invention. You can also negotiate sales-only or manufacturing-only licenses. Another option, put forth by inventor and marketer Bob DeMatteis, is creating a job for yourself within another company. As an in-house product development manager, you can develop your patent as an employee who receives a salary and stock options instead of royalties. (DeMatteis 1997, p. 19) The possibilities are truly limited only by your creativity, powers of persuasion and personal goals.

It's difficult to sell or license your invention unless it is patent pending or patented, though in rare cases you might be able to sell or license it as a trade secret, or as some other form of intellectual property. Most business deals involve an exchange—I'll give you this and you'll give me that. The rights granted to you by a patent give you something tangible to sell or license, and they prove that the invention is yours to sell. That said, though Knud Dyby, the paper clip dispenser inventor, didn't obtain a patent, he did profit from his invention. The injection molder who advised him against getting a patent did recognize the value of the invention. He manufactured the product and shared a percentage of the profits with the inventor.

There are a number of advantages to running your own business and/or overseeing your own manufacturing; you control quality, you maximize your profits (although these can also be substantial with savvy licensing) and you can pursue product improvements and additions as you see fit. Of course, starting a company requires the necessary business skills, lots of time, and a stomach for risk taking, not to mention the need for startup capital (see Chapter 2).

Potential problems to bear in mind are that a company that manufactures and sells only one product is sometimes a low priority for prompt payment from distributors, wholesalers and retailers. Also, it can be hard to sell just one product in a field; this continues to hinder the success of Zip Notes™. The corporate buyers we approach ask to see our catalog, expecting us to offer a range of office products. We don't. If our sales force represented a variety of products, we might be better able to offer promotional incentives.

In the 1980s I developed a highly successful game called Tangoes®, based upon the ancient Chinese Tangram puzzle. Tangoes® is a small and portable game for two. Each player gets seven geometric shapes that they rearrange to form different pictures. Whoever is first to match the picture on a card wins. I originally pitched a license deal to Parker Brothers, Ideal Toys and Hasbro, Inc. They all turned me down. I decided to form my own company (Rex Games) to manufacture and sell Tangoes®. We did this because we learned that we could go into stores and successfully sell the game ourselves. It was a great success, with sales far exceeding what Parker Brothers had forecast. We developed an entire catalog of Rex Games products by the time we sold out, but even with Tangoes® alone, we found we could get people's attention and make sales. Partly this is because the toy industry is much more open to fledgling companies if they have what looks like a hot product. In many fields, this is not the case and licensing would be much more prudent.

Deciding which moneymaking route to pursue depends partly on you—your interests and skills—and partly on your product. Are you entering an industry in which it's better to take advantage of an established corporation with existing distribution networks, research and development departments, a well-known marketing presence and financial resources—or does your product have a better chance for success and future growth on its own, guided by your unique vision?

Don Debelak, who has helped dozens of inventor/entrepreneurs market their new products, believes that solid products aimed at a small market are the most feasible to manufacture and market on one's own because without a big potential such products can become "lost in the shuffle" in a big company. (Debelak 1997, p. 63) I'm better off that Parker Brothers passed on Tangoes®. They had estimated sales at a hundred thousand units per year which wasn't enough for them, but if I sold it myself and made $1.50 profit on each, that was $150,000 per year. That was fine by me. In actuality, within a couple years we were grossing nearly $2 million a year. Taking the risk myself was not only profitable but also led to the creation of an interesting and enjoyable company, which I hadn't foreseen at the start. In addition, as Debelak stresses, you don't really need to make strict either/ or manufacturing and licensing decisions. Inventors who go into business for themselves can still make all kinds of strategic alliances with others—to distribute, market, manufacture and so on—that fall outside the traditional licensing arrangements in which the inventor prototypes, patents, makes a deal and moves on.

I have let my inventions dictate their most advantageous route to the marketplace. I was confident that I could produce, distribute and market the D-Fuzz-It® effectively. I understood the materials needed and educated myself about the intricacies of production. I even designed my own packaging and was confident that retailers would want to stock the product if I could get samples into their hands. I took a similar route with Tangoes® and, as we'll see in Chapter 5, with SKYY® Vodka. I believe I could do the same with Zip Notes™ if I had time to focus on it myself, or could find and hire someone with a management mindset more like mine.

Conversely, I am not the most effective marketer for my medical devices. These products need what a Johnson & Johnson or Becton Dickinson can provide: the ability to mass-produce intricate designs, a strong and reputable market presence, and established distribution and sales channels.

It never crossed my mind to manufacture my needle protector on my own, and I might have done better with the Kanbar Target and ROLLOcane if I had formed a licensing arrangement with such an entity.

Another thing you must consider is the cost of production weighed against a potential retail price. You can bet that any potential licensees will be looking at this closely for themselves. How much will people pay for your product in the marketplace? I don't use any hard and fast pricing formulas. Being able to retail for approximately four times your cost, including manufacturing, packaging, insurance, returns, waste, etc., is a standard goal ($1 to make, $3.98 retail). I'm sometimes willing to work with less of a markup because I have less overhead than people who maintain large payrolls and conduct expensive ad campaigns.

## HIRING A MANUFACTURER

Even if you handle distribution and marketing yourself, you probably won't set up your own manufacturing plant. The typical route that I've followed if I haven't licensed is to research and develop a product, apply for a patent and then hire someone to make a mold. (If you can't afford the mold, offer to pay the manufacturer a higher per piece price if he'll front you the mold.) I then own the mold and can take it elsewhere if I ever become dissatisfied with the manufacturer who made it, as you saw with the Rollit® fiasco. When 3D printing eventually becomes a commonplace manufacturing technique, make sure to retain ownership of the digital design and production files—they are easier to move around and copy than any mold.

I've sometimes contracted with another entity to assemble and package the manufactured parts (a veterans' organization that provided such work actually assembled the early D-Fuzz-Its®, and my overseas manufacturer assembled and even packaged Rollit®). Then it's time to either represent and sell the product yourself, or seek out a distributor (more on distribution in our SKYY® discussion as well).

## SOME WAYS TO FIND A MANUFACTURER

- *Ask someone with experience in the industry.*

- *Work your network: ask friends, colleagues, and their associates*

- *Work your LinkedIn online network, and participate in LinkedIn Groups that are pertinent to your product and industry.*

- *Go to industrial and trade shows.*

- *Read trade publications. Manufacturers will advertise.*

- *Contact local inventor associations and chambers of commerce.*

- *Ask an industrial designer for leads.*

- *Go to stores and research who manufactures similar items that are already being sold.*

- *Ask your potential retail or industrial customers for a recommendation.*

- *Look in the* Thomas Register *(in print or online, www. thomasregister. com).*

- *Let your fingers do the walking—through the* Yellow Pages.

- *Consult embassy trade development councils for manufacturers in other countries.*

> ## *If you want your eggs hatched, sit on them yourself.*
> **HAITIAN PROVERB**

Most often, inventors seek out domestic or overseas manufacturers who can meet their needs, craftsmen who are expert at making a product to a client's specifications for an agreed-upon price. Even so, you must become an expert in order to work with experts. Learn the terminology, understand the processes and know the materials.

You'll want to evaluate a manufacturer's quality and consistency. Examine other products they have produced. If you have any questions about their finances, ask to see an annual report or profit-and-loss statement. What is their reputation for service, commitment and innovation?

When you interview manufacturers, ask them to sign a nondisclosure agreement and/or have a patent in place or pending. Get references and price quotes. Can they deliver at your target price? Especially when working with overseas manufacturers, triple-check the production and shipping time. Do all you can to check into the company's good reputation and ethical business practices. Resist being talked out of the product quality and attributes you want. I persisted and insisted on top-quality plastic for the Tangoes® case, special inks and finishes for the SKYY® label and a certain type of chocolate for Vermeer. Your product should be market oriented, not production driven. When you make sales or get order commitments, draw up production contracts with your manufacturer with the help of your attorney.

If you do set up manufacturing capabilities of your own, remember to scale your production to the size of your market so that you don't tie up more funds than you need to in people, equipment or inventory.

## HOW TO MAKE IT EVEN BETTER

If you build your own business around your product, you will want to stay alert for opportunities to improve that product. The obvious goal is to keep customers happy—and purchasing. Throughout your initial product development and testing, you made modifications to meet the market's criteria. This doesn't end when your product is selling.

Of course, listen to your customers first—they'll tell you what improvements they'd like to see. But even if sales are humming along, you'd be wise to consider product modifications that keep you ahead of your competition and that maintain or add to your product's appeal. Over the years, I've improved SKYY® Vodka, achieving ever-lower levels of impurities. No one told me to do so, but I knew it could be done and could only boost our reputation. Doing so upped the ante for our competitors before they even came to the table. I made product improvements to Zip Notes™ that led to additional patents that extended my proprietary position.

Expanding a product line—as we did with additional Tangoes® versions and with SKYY® Citrus—is another way to offer consumers something new and to continuously generate attention and interest. From a marketing perspective, product improvements and variations also increase your market presence, often quite literally by requiring more shelf space. Considering how you can make your product even better is every bit as important after you've established your product as it was during your initial innovation. But never assume something is better just because it's different—only make modifications that genuinely improve the final product.

## MAKING A DEAL: WHEN TO LICENSE

As Edwin Bobrow notes, "Thomas Alva Edison died a wealthy man... [But] he did not die as wealthy as he should have. Much of his fortune was plowed into 'inventing' one new company after another and fighting legal battles associated with them. Somebody should have talked to him about licensing" (Bobrow 1997, p. 237).

Most inventors today don't need that talk. They already know about licensing, and for some, it is their only goal: they are quite happy to exchange their right to make and sell their invention for a healthy fee and a fair royalty. How do you achieve this? It's up to you to pursue the companies you hope will sign those royalty checks. First, we'll talk about making your pitch to prospective companies, and then we'll review all the aspects of a standard licensing deal and its main variations.

You can make your case to a company most effectively when your invention has been reduced to practice and you have something real to show them. You'll make your case most safely when your invention is patented or patent pending. When patents are not involved, remember those nondisclosure agreements.

But bear in mind that nondisclosure agreements are not ideal. If you feel yours has been violated, you must incur the expense of suing for damages. And companies are sometimes reluctant to sign them. What then? Consider disclosing "around" your secrets. Can you convey what your invention does and why it will be profitable without revealing all of its mechanisms? Having heard this much, the other party may be so curious that they become willing to sign your confidentiality agreement. But even if you proceed without a signed agreement, you can establish an implied confidential relationship that can provide you with some legal protections. (See Nolo Press's online legal encyclopedia at www.Nolo.com for more on this.) This occurs in several ways:

- *If the entity you are giving confidential information to solicits it from you without your prompting.*

- *If you make clear that you are presenting your invention as a business proposition and are looking for payment.*

- *If you request that they keep the information secret, and/or if the information is a trade secret with commercial value that is not known to competitors.*

- For a fee, the Patent and Trademark Office will publish a notice in their official gazette that your patent is available for licensing.

Research a potential licensee's track record, even if they are large and established. Look for a company that is familiar with your type of product; they may have to do less retooling of their own manufacturing process to incorporate it into their business. Look for one that does high-quality work and markets efficiently. Companies that don't maintain large and active research and development departments of their own may be more open to outside inventors and inventions like yours.

You can research companies through a number of routes:

- *Online, through company websites and LinkedIn*

- *Your local library: Reference librarians are trained to help you zero in on what you need and they typically know all the business directories, both national and local*

- *Trade shows*

- *Trade magazines*

- *Industry and trade associations: many publish member directories*

- *The Thomas Register: Supplier Discovery & Product Sourcing*

- *Standard and Poor's online*

- *Hoover's Business Directory from Dun & Bradstreet (online only)*

Contact the companies you are considering approaching and request literature, brochures and catalogs. Websites vary from one company to the next, with some sites being crammed full of useful information and others kept rather sparse. Public companies tend to have more information posted publicly as a result of SEC disclosure requirements, but that material is often heavily targeted at investors, not inventors. You may need to read very carefully to spot the information you need.

Once again, be wary of invention marketers who charge large fees, promise to find you the perfect "sugar daddy" licensee, and tell you not to worry about the details. What are their credentials? What is their matchmaking success rate? Do they want a big up-front fee and a hefty chunk of your royalties? Can they prove they have contacts you don't? There are legitimate invention marketers, but even if you employ one of them, you should educate yourself about every aspect of your invention and its potential.

Pitching your product in person is preferable to doing so through email, online, or through postal mail. To get an appointment with a company you've determined might be a good match for your invention, call the company and, depending on its size, ask for the president, the marketing director, or the person responsible for marketing your type of product—not the engineering or research and development departments. Identify yourself and why you are calling—because you have a new sticky note dispenser that would fit nicely into the company's product line, for instance.

I suggest you send a short letter requesting an appointment. Let them know you'll be following up by phone in a few days and then do so. You might also consider sending a brief product summary and pitch, but a personal presentation and a hands-on demonstration of your working model is much more effective. These days everyone is so accustomed to email, attached files, and remote real-time presentations that to offer to actually be present in person is something of a novelty and may get you a more positive response.

You can usually get your foot in the door to make your pitch. Many companies see bottom line value in discovering and developing great new products. How do they know you haven't got the next Frisbee? I was easily able to show Tangoes® to Parker, Ideal and Hasbro, even though I'd never created a game before. If you don't have a track record with the company or in the industry, a low-level employee may see you, but in any industry where many of their products come from outside inventors, you can usually be seen by someone. You can always poke around online, work your network, and get yourself introduced to an important executive through LinkedIn.

As I've said, when it comes time to pitch your invention, I have found that it's always best to have a working model rather than a crude mock-up or drawings. Partly this is because a "finished" product is always more impressive. But mainly it demonstrates your seriousness and professionalism, and if your invention is accompanied by a patent or patent pending, you show that you've done your legwork and aren't a daydreamer who thinks someone else can turn your idea into an invention with a little time, money and effort. Part of your appeal is that you have done the research and development work—you've done the hard part. Big established companies tend to be slow, lumbering and bureaucratic about introducing new products. If you have something that works, that they need in their product line and that you've developed to a working state, you truly have something to offer them.

Your presentation or pitch should do several things:

- *Show that your product has a sizable audience. Be specific about your target market and its size. Realistically estimate yearly sales and profit. Detail the product and market research you have done (outline your product's Ten Commandments) and the ways you have modified and improved your product based on testing feedback.*

- *Prove that your product is marketable. A good name can be helpful in this regard. Have you sold the product in a limited test market? If you are seeking a manufacturing partner, can you show that you have distributors waiting in the wings or retailers ready to buy?*

- *Explain how the product fits into the company's overall goals—which you've researched before pitching. Tell them why you have chosen them as a potential partner. Becton Dickinson, in addition to being our first choice for the needle protector for other reasons, was motivated to maintain their reputation for offering pioneering safety devices. We knew our product matched their industry profile.*

- *Demonstrate that the product will be easy to distribute.*

- *Convince them that your product is better than what they've come up with themselves. BD was already selling safety needles; ours was better.*

- *Anticipate any problems your product might encounter and show how you've designed around them.*

If there is a compelling, amusing, or otherwise interesting story behind the development of your idea, briefly tell it. Keep your pitch short. Use visual aids if appropriate—your model, most importantly. Show that you've done your homework, but don't bore listeners with every detail. You can bring attractively arranged and presented written information to leave with them, including any documentation that backs up your assertions.

If your product is rejected, politely ask why so that you can do better with your next pitch. They may point out flaws in your design, and you should consider these carefully. But don't run out and change your design or your mold just to suit them; their requirements or expectations may be unrealistic, and other companies could be very pleased with it as it is.

## WHAT'S THE DEAL?

If your talks with a company proceed, the conversation will come around to what sort of deal you're looking for. There are two basic options: you can sell your patent outright for an agreed-upon price with no future royalties (which I have never done), or you can strike a licensing deal whereby you retain ownership of your patent while allowing the company to make, use or sell the invention in exchange for royalty payments for an agreed-upon period of time. It is at this point that you'd do well to involve your attorney, especially if he or she is a savvy negotiator. The deal you are being offered may contain provisions that are not in your best interests and which you may be able to negotiate out of the deal. In order to do that, you'll need to understand any legalese in the proposed deal. I can't think of a situation when the goal of getting the best possible deal for yourself wouldn't be furthered by a consultation with your trusted patent attorney.

*"Do not, under any circumstances, assign [transfer ownership of] your patent in return for a series of payments: if your assignee defaults on the payments, you'll be left without your patent or your money, but with a big legal headache—getting your patent back. If someone wants to buy your patent for a series of payments, see a lawyer or legal forms book and make a suitable license with an agreement to assign only after all payments have been made."*

**DAVID PRESSMAN, PATENT ATTORNEY AND AUTHOR,** *PATENT IT YOURSELF* **(PRESSMAN 1997, CH. 16, P. 14)**

Negotiated royalties for licensing deals generally fall between 1% and 10% of the product's factory price, the money received by the manufacturer when it sells your invention-based product. They vary from industry to industry. Regardless of the industry, some factors that will influence your negotiations are whether you are providing an exclusive or non-exclusive license, how developed your product is, the competition it will face in the marketplace, the size of the licensing territory and so on. You can negotiate a staggered royalty that will increase after $x$ number of units have been sold. Royalty rates may also take the form of a flat rate, say $1 a unit.

If you can, negotiate a minimum annual royalty, which means that the last of the year's quarterly payments must add up to at least the agreed-upon minimum. These are desirable for many reasons, including the fact that they encourage the licensee to manufacture and sell your product, since they have to pay you your minimum even if they don't sell one widget. My needle protector licensing arrangement made this provision. Also attempt to negotiate that any up-front sum you receive for signing an agreement not be termed an advance against future royalties. It should instead represent payment for the work you've already done.

And give yourself an exit strategy. Our needle protector license specified that if BD didn't produce the product within a specified amount of time, the patent would revert to us and we could take it elsewhere. Remember Mary and her windshield wiper? She should have included a clause like this.

It's also possible, and preferable, to specify that if the licensor and licensee cannot resolve any dispute that arises under the license, mediation and/or arbitration will be sought and be considered final and binding. Court litigation is expensive and independent inventors generally do not have resources comparable to those of their licensees. I use binding arbitration agreements as a matter of course.

It is not unheard of for a company to enter into a licensing agreement with an inventor in order to eliminate his or her invention as competition. If you make a royalty-only deal, and the licensee never makes and sells the product, you don't see a dime. If a company professes to want to make a deal but resists anything but a royalty-only deal, it's possible their aim is simply to keep your product off the market.

While the amount of your royalty is an important part of your license agreement, it's only one of many issues. A well-negotiated license agreement ensures that you are paid fairly, it defines your rights and any limitations on the licensee, and it establishes what will happen as changes come up in the future. A comprehensive license agreement will cover all of the following areas:

- *Whether the license is exclusive or non-exclusive. Manufacturers will prefer exclusivity and my licenses have all been exclusive. A non-exclusive deal, which means that you retain the right to also license others, is standard when very valuable technology is involved. For instance, three Bell Labs inventors invented the transistor. The inventors won the Nobel Prize. It was a momentous, far-reaching discovery.*

- *Bell Labs licensed anyone who wanted to make it. They even taught people how to make transistors.*

- *How long the license will be in effect. Most licensees will want the life of the patent. While licensing for shorter periods of time may give you the right to renegotiate, you will want the license to last for as long as the product is being sold. A long-term relationship under fair financial terms is fine.*

- *A definition of the product to be licensed and whether its subsequent variations, derivatives and modifications are included in the agreement. It's in your best interests to obtain this broad wording, just as broad claims in your patent are in your best interests.*

- *The geographical and market scope of the license, such as the U.S. and kitchenwares. You may want to make these kinds of specifications if you intend to make separate deals overseas or in different industries, licensing your newly invented fiber to different companies for use in apparel, sporting goods, etc., for example.*

- *Whether you are willing to give the licensee the rights or right of first refusal to future inventions. This is restrictive for inventors.*

- *Your right to audit the company's books. While I've never taken advantage of such a clause, no reputable company should refuse to have one in their agreement.*

- *Who is responsible for pursuing patent infringements? You'll likely want to avoid being held responsible for pursing infringers—it's expensive to do so.*

- *Any agreed-upon rights to sublicense. The licensee should need your permission to make such arrangements—you'll want to negotiate how to share the profits of any such deals.*

- *Provisions for the licensee's bankruptcy or company sale. You want the right to terminate the agreement in either event.*

- *Finally, you should always have your attorney draw up your agreements, or at the very least have an attorney review them before signing.*

> *As a small businessperson, you have no greater leverage than the truth.*
>
> **PAUL HAWKEN**

When I developed an improved instrument for treating varicose veins, you'll recall that I invested in a mold with which to make samples. I gave samples to the doctor friend who had first spoken to me about vein-stripping procedures. He gave some samples to some of his colleagues and one way or another, Johnson & Johnson wound up calling me—not, I'm sorry to say, the usual way things work when you seek to license. Johnson & Johnson requested a meeting with me. At that initial meeting they asked if I could give them 150 samples to test market. Because I had made the mold, I could.

Johnson & Johnson got a terrific response and quickly called me back in. I had travel plans and asked if we could meet later in the month. They asked me to rearrange my plans and come in pronto. I did and we quickly made a lucrative deal, including up-front money and a nice royalty. "What was the big rush?" I asked them afterward. They explained how long it would have taken them internally to get to the production state my model was already in. They even admitted I could have asked for more up-front money. I didn't mind. Knowing from my physician friends that the need for my invention was great, knowing that my invention could be manufactured relatively cheaply and easily, and taking the time and trouble to develop and protect my invention had already paid off.

A final thought about pitching your invention and negotiating your deal: You will have fewer problems if you commit to being scrupulously honest. This may sound naive from a lifelong businessperson, but I'm quite serious. If you go into situations with nothing to hide, business—and life—is much easier. Don't inflate your claims for your invention or for the money you think it can make. If you are thinking that you have to pretend, or outwit, or fiddle with the facts, you constantly have to worry about being found out. It's so much easier to be direct and look people straight in the eye. Give what you hope to get in return—and accept nothing less from the people you work with. If everything about a deal you are being offered sounds great, but the man or woman on the other side of the desk won't look you in the eye and doesn't directly answer your questions, think twice. Be assured that any company president or executive worth his or her salt will be evaluating you the same way.

## THE COMING 3D REVOLUTION IN MANUFACTURING

As described in Chapter 2 "Prove Your Invention/Build a Prototype," 3D printing is really shaking things up. I think it is great for prototypers, but its effect on manufacturing has yet to be seen. Speculation is that it will eventually turn everything upside down, and I tend to agree. Emphasis here on "eventually."

3D printing is still in its infancy, but it's growing at an astounding rate, similar to how mobile technology has mushroomed since 2000. It is still used primarily by prototypers (in companies large and small), experimenters and hobbyists, but is poised for explosive growth in the industrial sector. President Obama called it out in his 2013 State of the Union address[1] as a means of reducing the costs of production here in the United States, putting U.S. workers back into jobs, and revitalizing the manufacturing sector. If you can create something cheaply here there is little to be gained by going overseas for it. Many things could be produced one at a time as needed and where needed, avoiding the need for extensive warehousing and wasteful transportation. And believe me, there is a lot of cost tied up in warehousing and transportation. I also like the thought of reduced manufacturing costs because that means that my philanthropic efforts either cost me less for the same result, or I can do more on the same bankroll.

3D printing can create just about anything, in plastic, metal, ceramic and even conductive materials. Visionaries say we could potentially print up a robotic toy monster in one go, including authentic scaly skin, articulated limb joints, a circuit board, and speaker for authentic roaring sound effects. Batteries sold separately.

Some 3D manufacturing scenarios I can think of include…

- *A factory with no molds but with dozens (hundreds?) of 3D printers all lined up and producing thousands of the same item, to be shipped for sale in retail stores. This is a likely early incarnation, considering the interest established manufacturers will have in staying in business. Economic forces will require them to install the most competitive technology within their existing infrastructure.*

- *The same factory with each machine producing different items, potentially ordered by different people. This is a kind of Amazon.com model, where one or two central facilities accept and process orders from all over.*

- *Small local shops equipped with printers of various sorts, accepting orders from local customers and producing the quantity requested on demand. You'd drive over and pick up your new wastebasket rather than buying it at Costco.*

- *Consumers buying and running their own 3D printers, much as they do laser or inkjet printers today. Folks would download design files online, buy the right types and colors of raw material to feed the printer, and manufacture what they need right at home. This model is being researched seriously for use aboard spacecraft.*

## HOW DOES THIS AFFECT YOU, THE INVENTOR?

Your combined creativity, curiosity, and vision will remain your greatest asset. Your digital files will be a close second. There will be increased risk of product piracy, as there has been with digital music and movies, simply because files can be copied and moved around with such ease. Unscrupulous producers may make a business of obtaining digital files of products they can produce and sell. The cyber security of your systems and your manufacturer's will become more important. It is also hard to control how many copies have been produced from a digital file. If they haven't already, I am sure some enterprising programmer will come up with security features to help prevent people printing from unlicensed copies of your files. Your legal agreements and NDAs with manufacturers will need to be re-written to cover their use and protection of your digital files. Perhaps "hacker insurance" will become a norm.

You'll be able to affordably produce parts for your product, if not the whole thing. The plastic case and certain internal parts of the Zip Notes™ machine could be produced this way, with workers installing motor, cutting blade, and other parts separately. In the next "printer-optimized" version perhaps the metal cutting blade and conductive parts for the push button switch will be printed in place, depending on the quality of material required and the capabilities of the printing machine. I still don't see the ability to print up a motor, with its internal magnets, bearings, copper wire windings and carbon brushes, but if someone can invent a printable motor of the right size and power you can bet I'll re-design Zip Notes™ to accommodate it. And I doubt they will be able to print batteries, so those will be sold separately.

The idea of every household printing up their own consumer goods is the futurist's ideal vision. Realistically, most people will not want, be able to afford, or have the skills to operate their own 3D printer, at least not in the near future. Commercially manufactured goods will be around for some time to come, I assure you. No machine outside of Star Trek will be whipping up a package of SooFoo™, a can of house paint, a microfiber pillow or a new Lexus, at least not in my lifetime. Local retail stores may eventually take a hit, as they have with the growth of online shopping, but it's probably not yet time to cash out your Wal-Mart stock.

If you have a small and simple invention, like a paperclip dispenser box or a plastic bacon rack for the microwave, you may eventually find it more profitable to just sell the digital files for it and let folks produce them at home. You may never actually go into production yourself. Such items are easily created on small 3D printers and should cost a lot less than selling retail. The more complex your invention, the less likely this will be. Even the paper clip dispenser would require the purchase and installation of a special magnet. Anything with motors, springs, magnets, lenses, and other special materials may require additional purchasing and assembly that the average person will not want to do. Will someone be able to print a pair of scissors at home? Considering the quality of steel and complex grinding required, I doubt it. But some might argue differently. Recent articles have described how people have successfully printed up their own functional firearms on home machines, so obviously the sophistication of home-printed items is increasing dramatically.

What about enterprising individuals cutting into your profit by scanning your product and reproducing it on a 3D printer? This is legal for some things, and illegal for others based on copyright, patent, and trademark law. I am not going to get into that here. Simpler inventions are easier to copy. But even a fairly simple machine like Zip Notes™ includes a motor, specialized drum, switch, cutting blade and internal workings that are tedious to replicate and assemble. Any consumer will find it easier to just order a Zip Notes™ machine and spare notepaper roll online. One-off copies that cheat you out of a sale are exceptionally unlikely and if someone manages it, you should congratulate them on their initiative and hire them as your next product developer. 3D scanning and printing may make it easier for a competitor to violate your patent and go into production, but they could do that with traditional techniques anyway.

It's currently 2013. For now, and the next few years, machining and molding still rule. Unless you plan to be a manufacturing pioneer, I would guess that over the next ten years 3D printing will influence your inventing experience more in the prototype phase than in manufacturing. I'll write a Third Edition of this book after the digital manufacturing shakeout, if I even live that long.

## (ENDNOTES)

1    http://www.cnn.com/2013/02/13/tech/innovation/obama-3d-printing/index.html?hpt=hp_bn5

# 5.

# Market with a Twist
You Go to My Head: SKYY Vodka

It may have started with a hungry caveman who'd had a bad day of hunting. Famished, he came upon some rotting, fermenting fruit and made a meal of it. It tasted pretty good and made him feel fantastic. He got such a nice buzz he forgot about the deer that got away. Soon he began waiting for fruit to spoil before eating it. He'd stumbled upon alcohol.

I've long enjoyed red wine with a meal, or a nice cognac after dinner. I like the way a drink with friends helps me unwind and makes me forget about the metaphorical deer that got away. I find alcohol—in moderation—to be a great stress reducer.

But like many people, I often experienced a downside after drinking. While many suffer a hangover the morning after, I was prone to pounding headaches a few hours after just a drink or two. I mentioned this to my physician friend Martin Sturman. He advised me to stay away from "brown goods" (bourbons, cognac and so on) and to stick with clear spirits like vodka. "They're less irritating," he explained.

> *Want, the mistress of invention.*
>
> **SUSANNAH CENTLIVRE, ACTRESS AND DRAMATIST**

So I switched to having a vodka martini or a screwdriver, and I did notice that I got fewer headaches. But one night at a dinner party, I had a cocktail-hour vodka—and was served a notable a headache before dessert. Martin was there, so I cornered him and said, "What's the deal? I'm drinking vodka and still got the headache." His diagnosis: My vodka came from a batch with a high "congener content."

A grown-up version of the kid who once hounded everyone with questions, I pestered my friend for more details. "What are congeners?" I asked. "And what are they doing in my vodka?"

"Congeners are by-products of distillation," he explained. "They give color, flavor and bouquet. They're present in clear spirits to a lesser degree than in the colored ones, but even small amounts can irritate you."

I grabbed a cocktail napkin, asked him to spell the unfamiliar word and stuffed the note in my pocket.

When I got home, I took down my unabridged dictionary and looked up "congeners," but couldn't find it. This was way back before the Internet so the next day I went to a medical library, where I found lots of information about congeners. I even discovered that there is a Department of Alcohol Studies at Rutgers University that researches just such things.

What I learned is this; during the fermentation of grain, sugar or carbohydrates, a variety of impurities, or congeners, are formed. Ethyl alcohol is what we want, but when alcoholic products are not distilled sufficiently, we end up with amyl, butyl, propyl and isoamyl alcohol, plus acetaldehyde, ethyl formate and methanol. Though you may never have heard the word congeners, if you've learned to avoid things like red wine or champagne because they give you a headache, studies have shown that congeners may be to blame.

Much like that concrete wall pulling the fuzz balls off my sweater, this bit of information got me thinking: Could vodka be distilled with fewer congeners? Would such vodka spare drinkers the headaches and queasiness associated with even a mild hangover? Where could I get such vodka?

I talked to bartenders. They gave me the same advice Martin had: "Stick to clear spirits." I called distillery executives and found that most of them had never heard of congeners. Undeterred, I got hold of a chemist in a distillery lab. I said I wanted purer vodka, one that would irritate people less. This fellow knew all about congeners, acknowledged that the typical distilling process did produce vodkas with varying levels of impurities and admitted that, theoretically, what I was looking for was possible.

That's all I needed to hear. Like the nineteenth-century inventor of the dishwasher—a woman who said if no one else was going to invent such a machine she'd have to do it herself—and as with so many of my other inventions, I made SKYY® because I couldn't buy it.

While SKYY® is arguably my most successful and well-known invention, I followed the same basic steps in developing it as I had with ideas like the Quad. I observed a problem (headaches after drinking), studied it (congeners were likely the culprit) and realized that solving the problem (getting rid of congeners) would offer consumers a real benefit (less irritation). Once I felt confident my idea was solid, I knew I needed to invent a "model" that proved it.

Finding a distiller who was willing to try to meet my standards of purity wasn't easy. In fact, it took a lot of time and persistence. "Who are you?" they said when I approached them. They were used to working with the huge spirits companies. I also heard, "We don't need another vodka. There are plenty of vodkas." And over and over I was told, "There's no demand for a cleaner spirit. We've been making vodka this way for years." I finally found one who agreed to take me on—if I paid a premium price "CBD." I'd never even heard that term. It means cash before delivery. "Send me a check, and if it clears, we'll work with you," the distiller said. My initial goal had been to invent a unique process that cut the level of congeners to twenty-milligrams or less per liter. But once we began to make some real progress, the chemists from the distiller's quality-control department got excited about it and we kept working to refine the process. Ultimately we brought the congener levels to less than ten parts per million. (Towards the end of my time with SKYY® our levels were virtually undetectable.)

When we'd achieved the less-than-ten-milligram quality level, I was convinced I had a great product. I had proved we could create dependably clean and smooth vodka. But I knew I had no business without the right name. I considered this so important that I sat tight after perfecting my distillation process and didn't proceed any further for almost a year. I just couldn't find a name that clicked. It had to be simple, catchy and convey the difference between my vodka and the others on the market. Without it, there was no point in launching the product.

I have a panoramic view from my San Francisco apartment. One day as I stood at my window looking out at a spectacular, fog-free day, the beauty of the clear, intensely blue, only-in-San Francisco sky hit me. Bingo! That was it: Sky Vodka. It said it all—this vodka was clean and clear as the sky outside my window. Harley Procter had a similar naming epiphany. In 1878, Procter and Gamble's new White Soap was selling well. After a long search for a more distinctive name, Procter rechristened the soap Ivory upon hearing a snippet of the Forty-fifth Psalm ("out of the ivory palaces") during a Sunday morning church service (Panati 1987, p. 218), and greater success followed. Inspiration can strike anytime, anywhere. Amen.

Adding an extra "y" to "sky" gave the name a twist and made it even more distinctive. It worked for Exxon, didn't it? In 1992, nearly five years after my first research into congeners, I was finally ready to take my vodka into the marketplace.

Did I patent my distillation process before producing my "model" or entering the marketplace? No. Though we could have obtained a process patent from the Patent and Trademark Office, to do so would have made our unique process public and after the patent expired, anyone could have copied it. Our proprietary method of filtration is our trade secret. While Coca-Cola's name is trademarked, the script of its logo registered and even its classic bottle shape patent protected, their formula is not patented either. It's too valuable a trade secret. There are lots of wild stories about how Coca-Cola protects their formula. I protect mine by using confidentiality agreements and limiting the number of people who know the nuts and bolts. But the truth is that given the sophisticated technologies that exist today, most substances can be tested and understood quite precisely by anyone who wants to take the trouble to do so. The law offers some protection from this, and allows you to claim trade secret status, if you can show that you consistently make an effort to keep your secret, secret. (You need not file for or in any way register your trade secret.)

Getting a license to go into the alcohol business was surprisingly easy—basically a matter of filling out forms. But as usual, I heard "Are you crazy?" more than once. Friends and business associates said, "You can't go up against the big, established guys. They'll squash you like a bug!" I'd cleared the hurdle of producing vodka that met my stringent quality requirements, and I'd come up with a memorable name, but distributing SKYY®—actually getting it into stores, bars and restaurants—was the real challenge. How does an upstart outsider get into the game?

Since I had resources at my disposal, some people might assume I simply threw a ton of money at the problem of distribution, bought a lot of ads and that was it an instant success. It didn't happen this way because while money always helps, money is not what it takes to launch a product. Remember New Coke? Coca-Cola makes more money than many small nations. They were practically paying people to try New Coke, and still it flopped. The truth is, if you have a good product, have read the market correctly and are persistent in your efforts, you can succeed. Money is the result of success, not the cause of it.

I marketed SKYY®, when I had money in the bank, the same way I sold the D-Fuzz-It®, when I had no money to my name. Instead of getting discouraged when people told me I was making a big mistake and the odds of success were long, I put my faith in my product, got creative and personally delivered SKYY® to potential customers to convince them of its worth.

Remember that this was all before the Internet became a household appliance. There was no Facebook to help us spread the word and we weren't even equipped with email. More on the Internet later.

To begin, I hired three employees. My sales, publicity and office people worked out of a very small, no frills office. My salesperson and I hit the streets, visiting restaurateurs and bartenders all over the city. I got on my scooter and visited liquor stores. Since federal regulations set down by the Bureau of Alcohol, Tobacco and Firearms wouldn't allow me to sell on a consignment basis, I went in to retail establishments and made a personal pledge: "If you buy three cases at the wholesale price, I'll come back in a week and personally buy back at full retail price any bottle you haven't sold." In other words, I wasn't taking "returns." I was offering to buy the product just like any other customer. I believed in SKYY® that much, and that kind of belief is contagious. I wound up never having to buy a bottle of SKYY® at retail.

We spread the word about congeners and our nearly congener-free vodka. Bartenders were very receptive. Like any retailer, they like having something exciting to share with their customers. The stylish and health-conscious San Francisco gay community took to SKYY® immediately as well. You can't buy loyalty—you have to earn it. People may want to try whatever seems trendy and new, but they won't come back for more unless you make good on your promises. We did.

In this personal, one-to-one way, we forged relationships and made converts. A good name and a nice sales pitch can't hide a weak product. People can see through hype. If you have an honest, innovative item at a fair price—since SKYY® was made in America, we could sell it for significantly less than the premium imports—you can sell it. We knew we had something solid to offer, and just like those first D-Fuzz-It®s, our initial bottles of SKYY® proved our point. We got orders.

Still, a little free publicity couldn't hurt. The story of congeners and how they relate to that hangover feeling had been news to me. Though today you might pitch to leading bloggers or Facebook commentators, back then you went to the newspapers with news. We wrote a press release that told the SKYY®/congeners story and sent it to the local papers. In June of 1992,

# San Francisco Examiner

Sunday
JUNE 14, 1992

# Inventor shoots for pie in the SKYY

## Kanbar's vodka allegedly causes less pain

By Robert Shrer
OF THE EXAMINER STAFF

*Maurice Kanbar believed there were "sensitive drinkers" who could be enticed by a vodka that was free of headache-causing congeners.*

NOT TOO many good ideas come after drinking a couple of screwdrivers. Oh, you may think so at the time, but a decent headache has a way of replacing such thoughts. Maurice Kanbar felt that inevitable rise around his head about two years ago at a cocktail party, but for him, a thought came popping out.

Kanbar, an inventor by trade, considered the possibility of purifying vodka to the point where it would no longer cause a headache. Kanbar believed there were other "sensitive drinkers," that could be enticed by a vodka that was free of congeners, the toxic impurities that form during the fermentation process.

Using a distillation process in which the vodka is boiled at four different temperatures, Kanbar has developed a new product in the Bay Area market: SKYY Vodka.

"I just couldn't handle the side effects of certain alcohols," Kanbar said. "I love the feeling of drinking in moderation, though. It's probably the best natural sedative given to men, but I just couldn't drink brandy or bourbon because of the headache I'd get. And then when a white spirit like vodka gave me trouble, I became curious with the possibility of purifying it."

Kanbar, born in New York and a graduate of the Philadelphia College of Science and Technology, said his new process doesn't alter the alcohol content of the drink, just eliminate most of the congeners. The process isn't intended specifically for heavy drinkers, he said. Some people can get headaches from just one drink. And he isn't promising a hangover-free morning if you drink more quantities (you will still be dehydrated), but he said the headache will most likely be gone.

"Not everyone gets headaches from drinking, of course," he said. "Some people even think that congeners take give of the edge of the alcohol and give a drink character. This is intended for the 3 percent or so that are affected by the congeners."

Kanbar said he is always looking for the big breakthrough. He already has 30 patents to his credit including the "D-Fuzz-It," a little comb-like device that removes fuzz balls from sweaters. It may not sound like much, but Kanbar said sells about 300,000 a year to discount stores across the country.

He also has patented several surgical instruments including one for cataract cryogenic removal, where the lens of the eye is frozen and removed intact. He sold that to Alton Laboratories (a division of Nestle) in Austin, Texas. He also sold a type of surgical extractor used for various veins to Zimmer, a division of Bristol Myers.

"I look around all the time and just have a feeling that everything can somehow be improved to design," he said. "I mean, think of it. When we were kids we used to underline books with a pencil. Then some genius thought of highlighter pens. Another guy thought up Post-its. What brilliant ideas. Post-its did about $250 million in business last year. You don't have to be technologically brilliant to do this stuff. You just have to be alert."

Kanbar, single and living in The City, hopes the next great discovery will be his San Francisco-based SKYY Vodka. Distilled in Illinois and shipped to a bottling plant in San Jose, SKYY Vodka has found its way to about 60 locations in the Bay area including Pat O'Shea's in Geary, The Blue Light on Union, The Lone Palm on Guerrero and the Lark Creek Inn in Larkspur as well as several retail outlets. It's being distributed by Citizen Imports in Brisbane.

Jeff Jordan, owner and general manager for both the Blue Light and the Fillmore Bar and Grill said SKYY Vodka is slowly becoming a seller.

"The taste is real smooth," he said. "The response has been very positive. It's still a cult drink (used to be requested specifically), but we had a SKYY Vodka night a few weeks ago where we used it for all vodka drinks. We've been getting more and more people coming in and asking for it specifically. It's pretty competitively priced."

Word-of-mouth will have to be the primary marketing tool, Kanbar said, because the advertising budget is still very small. With four employees, SKYY Spirits Inc. first began marketing in San Francisco because "it was a large enough area to gain a following but still small enough where we could track the program," Kanbar said. He also named The City's reputation for quality living and high regard for good health.

Kanbar doesn't expect to turn a profit for at least two years. He can't patent the process, he said, because it is a concept and not an actual invention, but he sees big things ahead.

The plan for now is to move to Los Angeles in six months if all goes well. If the vodka takes off in California, Kanbar hopes to take it to New York.

That would bring him full circle. Kanbar, who is also on the board of directors for the San Francisco International Film Festival, grew up in New York and may have hit a big money venture only through his films.

"In 1972 I owned a building in New York and decided that what New York needed was a four-plex cinema. I coined the concept, but didn't expand it and didn't earn any money with it. I was just happy to have those theaters because I loved film so much. It's tough to look back on that now."

If his SKYY Vodka can make its way back to New York, it just might eliminate the bad taste in his mouth.

the *San Francisco Examiner* ran with it. A staff writer interviewed me and wrote an attention-grabbing story under the headline, "Inventor shoots for pie in the SKYY®." They even sent out a photographer and included a photo of me with a bottle of SKYY® in the story. Readers' curiosity was piqued and they began asking for SKYY® by name.

The only distributor we could get to work with us at the outset was a small imported beer distributor. We were not his top priority but as the publicity increased the demand for SKYY® grew, and there was a domino effect. The distributor got more orders.

*USA Today* picked up the story ("Vodka purified to cut hangovers"), followed by newspapers and magazines from the *Wall Street Journal* and *Newsweek* to *Details. Business Week's* story was headlined "Hangover-proof 80 proof?" I was invited to appear on local and national TV news programs on networks including CNBC and Fox. Before we knew it, David Letterman was grabbing a bottle of SKYY® that a guest chef was using in a cooking segment and guzzling it prominently on his Late Night television show. More orders.

In less than ten years SKYY® achieved annual sales of more than $50 million and became the number-two premium vodka in the U.S. We went from talking shopkeepers into giving us a square foot of floor space in their store to being courted by distributors anxious to do business with us. By the time we were done, SKYY® was sold in every state in America and in eighty countries. We raised the bar for the entire spirits industry, with competitors eyeballing our quality standards and imitating our marketing techniques. I guess you could say we shook things up.

In 2009 SKYY® was fully acquired by Campari Group of Italy. I can't comment on any marketing activities or product development that has occurred with SKYY® since then, so all my observations are about what we ourselves did with SKYY® while we still controlled it.

SKYY®'s success was rooted in the quality of the product itself, but naming, packaging and marketing also played a crucial role, as they do with any product. Once you have something worthwhile to sell, you need to convey that value to customers, preferably with a twist as distinctive and memorable as your product itself. Let's look at how we did that with SKYY®.

## FIRST IMPRESSIONS: NAME, PACKAGE, PRICE

What's in a name? Everything. Remember the hit movie from the 1980s, *Dirty Dancing?* Was it a success because it was a great film? No. The title brought people into the theater. I doubt they'd have come out for the same film if it were called *Weekend in the Catskills.*

Although I've never done it, I've often said that if I had a great name for a product, I'd build a business around the name. That's how important names are.

In 1965 I got a patent for a flat film dental floss that I'd invented. It slid between teeth easily and comfortably. I tried to sell it to Johnson & Johnson and Colgate but found no takers. I thought about manufacturing and selling it myself, but I couldn't come up with a snappy name—I kept calling it something clunky like Film Floss. Nowadays, Oral-B markets flat film floss called Glide. That's a terrific name. If I'd thought of it, or maybe even just Slide, I would have manufactured the stuff myself. Alas, my patent is long expired.

Unlike patents, names don't expire. That's one reason why they are so valuable. While the value of a patent tends to depreciate, since competitors can study your patent and begin to build on it, names appreciate. No one

> *A good name is rather to be chosen than great riches...*
> **PROVERBS 22:1**

else can use them, and over time they attract recognition and loyalty.

Sometime in the 1970s, long before you could find Evian and San Pellegrino at your corner store, I was eating at a restaurant in a small Georgia town. A man and his date were sitting at the table next to me and the man asked for a Perrier—not a "bottled water" or a "club soda," but a Perrier. I'd bet that the fellow was trying to impress his date with his discernment and sophistication. A French name that's easy to pronounce achieves a kind of cachet that has tremendous value for the manufacturer. People feel good about themselves when they buy the product, and other people notice and follow suit because they want that touch of class as well. It's brilliant marketing.

Names like that become part of the language. Do you make a copy or a Xerox, use tissues or Kleenex, apply petroleum jelly or Vaseline®? Those names are like gold.

Legally your product name is trademarked the first time it is used in public. You can use TM after your name from the first date of use. But you can use the ® symbol only after you've registered your name with the U.S. Patent and Trademark Office. This is simply a matter of filling out paperwork. The office then reviews your trademark and double checks that it is unique. You can file either a "use" application, if your trademark has already been commercially used, or an "intent-to-use" application. Trademarks may be registered only when they are used in interstate commerce; you need to show that you've sold the product to someone in another state. And commonly used words can't be trademarked; that's one of the reasons for SKYY®'s spelling. Trademark registration must be renewed every ten years, and a mark may be considered abandoned after two years of nonuse.

> • Sometimes you just get lucky. I decided I wanted to call my new chocolate cream liqueur Vermeer, and was warned that a lot of people might not have heard of the painter. In a few years following the product launch there suddenly were four very successful books concerning Vermeer. The best-selling 1999 novel Girl With a Pearl Earring even featured the same painting on the book jacket as we put on our label. The serendipity grew when an opera, Writing to Vermeer, by Peter Greenaway, played at Lincoln Center the week before we launched. In 2013 the original painting was on exhibition at San Francisco's de Young Museum and we did a few promotional events around that.

To make sure that the trademark you've chosen isn't already in use, you should do a search of both registered and unregistered marks. There are trademark search firms, directories are available in most libraries, and there are many search options online including TESS, the Trademark Electronic Search System offered by the USPTO. Unregistered marks can be researched in trade directories as well. (See appendix.)

Back when I was trying to name SKYY®, I toyed around with things like Prince Nikolai or Czar Alexander—obviously hung up on the Russian thing. But how many people would go to a bar and say, "Give me a Czar Alexander and tonic"? It's too complicated and sounds fussy.

Your product name has to sound right in just these kinds of real-life scenarios. You have to imagine your name being used in the situations your customers will find themselves in. I could hear that fellow in Georgia ordering a SKYY® martini, SKYY® Mary, SKYY®-driver, or SKYY®-hound, just the way I could hear a woman saying, "Let's go to the Quad." The right name clicks. (Unfortunately, I neglected to register "Quad." A rash of four-plexes sprang up after my success with the concept, and if I had registered the name, I could conceivably have collected licensing fees from my imitators. Learn from my mistake.)

I mentioned earlier that SooFoo™ is a shortened version of "super good food." It is unique, and it is easy to pronounce in conversation. Blue Angel is very easy and even pleasant to say, and it lends itself to alteration. A Blue Angel Martini becomes a BAM! A margarita made with our vodka becomes an Angelrita. A name can take you far.

Consider what image you want to convey. Clinique and Prescriptives are cosmetic companies whose names signal products with scientific benefits. But Urban Decay is also, believe it or not, a line of cosmetics. They feature nail polish colors like Uzi, just right for their target market: the Irony Generation.

I actually had my eyes on the name "Vermeer" before I had perfected the chocolate cream liqueur that would bear the name. I knew I wanted a rich, even sensuous drink. If you've ever seen a painting by the seventeenth-century painter Johannes Vermeer, you'll see the connection. Vermeer's work is warm, golden and suffused with light—it's every bit as sensuous as our drink. Plus Vermeer was Dutch, like the premium chocolate we use—and I've read that he was just as obsessed with details as I am. When I'm in New York, I regularly visit the Vermeers in the Frick Collection. We even recreated a detail from the Vermeer painting *Girl With a Pearl Earring* on our label.

Ordering Perrier at a bar or restaurant didn't become a classy and health-conscious thing to do in the 70s and 80s because of the bubbles. Its spring source, which is thought to be 130 million years old, was originally called *Les Bouillens*, or boiling waters. Napoleon III granted the rights to commercialize the spring in 1863, and the bottler had the good sense to call it Perrier, the name of the physician who headed the *Société des Eaux Minérales, Boissons et Produits Hygéniques de Vergéze*. When the venerable product exploded on the U.S. market in the mid-1970s, it capitalized on both its European sophistication and its natural, calorie-free health benefits. The company emphasized its "*hygéniques*" by sponsoring the New York Marathon and Los Angeles Olympic Games, and by creating its "Earth's First Soft Drink" tagline. Perrier's sleek, elegant and instantly recognizable green bottle added to its allure.

The first safe commercial hair dye was marketed in 1909 by the French Harmless Hair Dye Company. At first, the company moniker was also the product name, and while this conveyed important information about the product's quality, it obviously lacked something. A year later the name was changed to L'Oreal, and suddenly you knew your hair wasn't going to be just safely dyed but also glamorous. (Panati 1987, p. 233)

## TIPS FOR BRAINSTORMING A NAME

- *Make up a word (Oreo, Kodak)*

- *Consider positive image words (Eternity perfume, Renew recycled trash bags)*

- *Use a unique spelling of a common word (SKYY®), or a combination of words (Slim-Fast®, Pull-Ups®, Band-Aid®)*

- *Speak a foreign language, or pretend that you do (Tavolo.com, Frappuccino)*

- *Use scenarios—what will someone say, notice, remember*

- *Ask your friends—I overrode a friend's Movies 4 suggestion but another friend's idea spared the world the Balls Off sweater comb*

Vermeer, Perrier and L'Oreal add a touch of class, but there are no hard-and-fast rules for names. You can be more literal to convey a product's key benefits, such as Zip Notes™, Huggies Pull-Ups®, Slim-Fast®, Good Grips™, and Baby Jogger®. These names are snappier than "French Harmless Hair Dye," but their focus is still usefulness, concentrating on product features rather than glamour or style. With some products and in some markets, this is more appropriate.

Unfortunately, product naming has become very complicated because of the Internet. You have to choose a name that makes a good web address (or URL) so people can find you easily online. Ideally, your URL will be your company or product name followed by .com, which is the most widely used commercial address suffix. (Actually, ".com," ".net" and the other "dots" are known as "top-level domains.") Web addresses should also be short if possible. Thus, www.soofoo.com and www.zipnotes.com are great URLs, and those are what we use.

However, what if you have a great product name like Blue Angel, but someone else already has www.blueangel.com? That's what happened with us, but fortunately www.blueangelvodka.com was still available. In the world of business names and trademarks, you can generally use the same name as another company as long as you are in a sufficiently different industry. So calling our vodka Blue Angel does not infringe upon the tech company that owns www.blueangel.com, or on any other company not in the spirits or food industry. There are probably many companies in the world that use the Blue Angel name but there is only one www.blueangel.com address so only one company can get it. We were lucky that www.blueangelvodka.com suited us, though it is a little long. Similarly, you can find our Vermeer Chocolate Cream Liqueur at www.vermeercream.com. So before you get too hung up on a name, make sure a suitable URL is available or your marketing will become very difficult.

And speaking of infringement, you need to be careful of naming it too similarly to an existing product in the same general industry. I first launched Zip Notes™ as Rollit®, but a friendly note from 3M made it clear they felt it was too similar to their trademark Post-It®. I had the alternate name Zip Notes™ all lined up, so changing was not too traumatic, though we did need to re-do a bunch of packaging and marketing materials.

Once you decide on a URL, register it right away before someone else gets it. At a few dollars a year they're cheap, and you can afford to hang on to a good one for years if need be until you go to market. If the URL you want is already taken you might ask its owner if he'll sell it. This can get expensive, depending on its perceived value. You can also modify your URL, similar to how we added "vodka" to the end of ours. Options like "drinkblueangel," "tasteblueangel," "goblueangel" and others presented themselves, but "blueangelvodka" was the better of these second choices. You could register under one of the other top-level domains and use one of the other "dot" suffixes like .net or .org, but .com is so widely used for commercial ventures that it's best to use it. If soofoo.com had been taken and we chose soofoo.net, customers would never find us because they'd be too busy typing soofoo.com.

One note of caution: have a stranger look at your proposed URL to spot undesirable meanings. For example, the Dollars Exchange site is apparently a legitimate source of information about international currency values and such. However, their URL—www.dollarsexchange.com—seems to imply they offer services of an entirely different sort. If you are doing business overseas, have a native speaker look at your URL to make sure it contains nothing objectionable in their language.

> *Business has only two basic functions: marketing and innovation.*
>
> **PETER F DRUCKER**

With SKYY®, I wasn't exacting about just the name. It also took me months to come up with a better way to say "Made in America." I wanted

to let people know that my vodka wasn't Russian or Swedish, but the way
I said this was important to me. The phrase had to flow and have the right
cadence. I finally came up with "Distilled in America from American Grain."
Doesn't that sound better than "Made in the USA"?

These aren't minor details. They are an integral part of what makes a
brand distinctive. SKYY® went beyond its quality and low congener count,
it's got a simple, memorable name and it's American. You have to give people
an incentive to try your product, and then make it very easy and appealing
for them to stick with it. Give them reasons to explain their choice, make
them proud to order it.

## PERFECTING THE PACKAGE

If the name of the vodka is SKYY®, you can hardly put it in a green or
yellow bottle. As night follows day, the bottle should be blue.

But at the outset, I was cautious. Using a blue bottle wasn't going to be
easy or inexpensive, so I wanted to be sure of several things: Did I have a
truly fine product? Yes. Was there a market for the product?

To find this out, I distributed five thousand cases of SKYY® in a water-
clear glass bottle in the Bay Area, and spread SKYY®'s low congener/anti-
headache story. I had to prove that there was an audience, that people were
listening. By pounding the pavement, conducting taste tests, and telling our
story, I learned that drinkers did understand the value of SKYY® enough
to buy it in an unremarkable bottle. And our initial bottles were truly plain.
Sometimes after Dave Stoop, SKYY®'s first salesperson, and I did a taste
test with the bottle concealed in a brown paper bag, the potential customer
would say, "You're right, it's great. Now let me see the bottle." Some of
them grimaced when we revealed our generic, almost medicinal bottle.
But I was determined to test the value and salability of SKYY® on its own
merits.

Every Friday afternoon, I met with my employees in my office to recap
the week's events. Invariably the plain bottle would come up. "Please get
us a better bottle!" one would say. "First sell five thousand cases," I insisted.
Finally, when I realized our initial customers were loyal, I decided to pull

out all the stops and do whatever it took to get a blue bottle. Our limited, local initial sales and taste tests were essentially "end-user" trials. Our feedback told us that our customers liked everything except our bottle.

Still, because I was about to break with industry standards, I heard "Are you crazy?" all over again. Some people said, "The colored glass won't let you see how much vodka is left" or "No one uses a colored bottle for a clear spirit." Exactly. No one else was doing it. I knew the blue bottle would make SKYY® even more distinctive, and I was willing to bet that any minuses would be outweighed by the plus of having SKYY® truly stand out behind the bar or on the store shelf. I clung to my idea like a pit bull.

What's more, when I hear a businessperson say, "That's the way it's always been done," I bristle. If you've been doing something the same way for twenty-five years, I wonder why you aren't innovating—and I know that you're leaving yourself vulnerable to a competitor brave enough to try something new. Most of the time, when people say, "You can't do that," they mean, "It's never been done." That's not a good enough reason.

Where would Apple be if they didn't "think different" back in 1998 and put their iMac in colorful transparent housings? What if their design team had said, "We can't make colored computers because no one ever has?" Apple probably would not have enjoyed its historic revival and ensuing fifteen years of success. Of course, the iMac also had to be easy to use and competitively priced, but it was the translucent plastic colors that embodied their cutting edge style. And they kept it up, at least while Steve Jobs was still alive, by taking the all-in-one iMac idea to its logical next step, miniaturizing everything and putting it in one unit the size and configuration of a flat-screen monitor.

Jonathan Ive, the iMac industrial design team leader, said that his team approached their project with no preconceived notions of what a computer should look like. Before he was an Apple employee, he had been devoted to the Macintosh because of its "more emotive, less tangible product attributes." He brought that history to the iMac project, creating colors not just to differentiate the product in the marketplace, but also to "create products that people would love." Setting trends isn't incidental or accidental. At Apple, it's their MO. As Ive stated, "In a company that was born to innovate, the risk is in not innovating." (Hirasuna, 1998) What with the growth of the Internet and the vastly increased speed in which ideas are exchanged today, that is even more true than it was back when he first said it.

Despite my determination, obtaining a blue bottle for SKYY® was difficult. I could not find an American glass company willing to manufacture one for me. I learned early on that you should never refuse to do what a customer asks, even if it seems unreasonable. Rather than say, "No, that's too expensive" or "No, that's too much trouble," you should listen to the customer and then say, "This is what it'll take." Charge them for your time and trouble, of course, but do what they ask. You never know, if you go the extra mile for them, they might turn out to be your best customer.

I found a company in Hannover, Germany, that was making blue bottles for another customer. I had to pay them much more than I was paying for clear glass in the United States, but I was willing to do so and they were willing to work with me. This led to a long-term relationship and the stateside companies lost out on a big customer.

Just as Coca-Cola is recognized by its bright red label, SKYY® became identified with its distinctive cobalt blue. Not only did the bottle play off the name (sky blue), it also emphasized our lack of impurities (clear blue), and it stood out on the shelf. We introduced the blue bottle in 1993 and a year later it was featured on the cover of *Packaging World* magazine with an inside story headlined, "SKYY® Gets It Right." Two years after launching, we were enjoying 15% to 20% jumps in sales per month, due in no small part to the bottle improvement.

Imitation may be the sincerest form of flattery, but when new vodka brands were launched in blue bottles I was not amused. "Trade dress" is a distinctive but nonfunctional feature that distinguishes one product from others. As time goes by, unique and distinctive trade dress, like a trademark, becomes more valuable as a means of identification for the consumer. Also like a trademark, trade dress can be registered with the PTO. But it doesn't have to be in order to receive protection. If it's distinctive and consistent, and if an imitation could cause consumer confusion, unfair competition law—an admittedly gray and changeable area of the law—gives you offensive rights. If you bring suit, a judge could tell the other business to stop or modify their behavior and even award the injured business monetary compensation for lost profits.

For example, if I decided to go into the photographic film business, I couldn't package my film in a yellow box. That would invade Kodak's trade dress. Kodak owns that look. They could easily make the case that even if my film was called Glotz, if I packaged it in a copycat yellow box; I was attempting to confuse consumers into buying Glotz when they wanted Kodak.

One of our blue-bottle copycats called themselves Ultraa—they even copied the double letters in the name! But their bottle's shape was quite different from ours; it was curvy and voluptuous, so I didn't take any action. Another cobalt blue imitator used a bottle that at first glance could be mistaken for ours. I felt that was a trade dress infringement and was willing to go to court over it. Chances are good that a judge would have ruled in our favor, but we settled when the competitor agreed to sell out their current stock and then stop copying us. There's a time to be flattered, and trust that your customers will remain loyal, and there's a time to take action. Consumers had come to expect to find SKYY® Vodka in cobalt blue bottles, and we had a right to protect that.

> *Never leave well enough alone.*
> **RAYMOND LOEWY, INDUSTRIAL DESIGNER**

I could have hired a designer to create our new bottle, but I didn't. I have nothing against designers, not at all. But I'm picky and have a strong, gut-level sense of what does and doesn't work. At the beginning, with the D-Fuzz-It® for instance, I couldn't afford designers. I did my homework, went with my instincts, and the result was successful. That trained me to trust my gut and reinforced my do-it-yourself tendencies. For the Vermeer packaging, we did work with a designer. I had the name and the product image, and knew I wanted to recreate a portion of a Vermeer painting on the label, but I also wanted to stretch out and experiment a little. I felt I could afford to see what someone else could come up with and then direct the changes. The collaboration worked out very well.

But with SKYY®, I looked at various bottle shapes and chose an extremely simple, slim bottle with sloped shoulders. SKYY® was a direct, honest product. The bottle needed to reflect that simple elegance. If something is fussy and ornate, you are more apt to tire of it. Plus, an intricate bottle would have contradicted our clear and clean product. To position your product in the marketplace, and garner interest and excitement, the product, name, package and promotion should fit together seamlessly.

Speaking of bottles, until 1915, Coca-Cola came in a bottle that was very similar to those of other soft drinks. To give Coca-Cola drinkers a way to spot the product before their first sip, the company replaced their generic straight-sided bottle with their contoured one that could be recognized "even if it was felt in the dark." (www.cocacola.com) In 1977, in a move that was rare for the Patent and Trademark Office, Coke's unique bottle was granted registration as a trademark.

I did have a designer present me with some label mock-ups for SKYY®, but nothing she came up with felt right. So I went the D-Fuzz-It® route; that is, I chose the typeface, type sizes, and colors myself. But I did have one hell of a time getting the gold I wanted for our label.

In Jim Jarmusch's 1999 movie, Ghost Dog, a character talks about a tenet of samurai philosophy: you can put aside the really big problems but the small problems require a lot of attention. Next time someone tells me I'm too finicky, I'll tell them I'm a bit of a samurai because I have always found that the "little" things add up and matter.

I kept telling the printer we were working with on the SKYY® label that I wasn't happy with the quality of the gold lettering. He thought I was nuts. (Join the crowd.) The problem was that if you looked at the label from a certain angle, the gold took on a distinctly green tinge. I didn't want that. The printer said there was nothing he could do about it. "It's fine. No one is going to look at it from the side." But I looked at it from all sides, and it bothered me.

One day I noticed a gold can of caffeine-free Coca-Cola. I had learned that that look is achieved with transparent yellow ink. You can take paper and vaporize, or vacuum deposit, a very thin coat of aluminum on it and the paper ends up looking metallic. If you print over that with transparent yellow, it looks gold. If the yellow has some red in it, it looks like copper. The Duracell copper battery is in a steel case that is printed with a transparent yellow-red so that it looks like copper.

So I'm holding this can of Coke and thinking, "Now there's a gold; there's no green in that." With this validation that what I wanted could be done, I made some calls and found the manufacturer of the ink Coke used. Inks, Inc., turned out to be just across the bay from me, in Oakland, California. Confronted with the evidence, my printer said, "Okay, okay. You're right. We can make that gold for you."

> • Consider placing a bulletin board notice up at a local art school or college.
> You might be able to obtain high quality design help at reasonable rates
> from a student.

But that wasn't the end of my label woes. Our first labels got scuffed by the cardboard separators in their boxes and in normal handling. I was told this was to be expected, that it was no big deal, and that it would only happen to one out of every thirty or forty bottles. What's the big deal if two or three out of a hundred bottles are imperfect? The trouble is, if a person picks up a bottle, sees the scuff, and puts the bottle back on the shelf, you'll eventually wind up with six scuffed bottles on the shelf. Remember to think even the smallest things through to their logical conclusion—do the scenario. I insisted on scuff-resistant labels.

I first tried having the labels coated with special transparent ink. But in order to become tough, the ink has to be exposed to ultraviolet light; the ink literally polymerizes and forms a thin plastic coating. The folks who did my coating did it so fast that it didn't really polymerize and didn't have the abrasion resistance that I wanted. After some more back and forth, I decided to laminate a thin film onto the label after it was printed. It was a little more expensive, but it worked. The SKYY® brand has changed a little over they years with its new owners, and the labels look a bit different and are printed differently, but that was how I got the look and performance I wanted.

This entire label perfecting probably took nine months. It's easy to be tempted to let some of these details go in favor of getting your product out there. But if you let them go, they have a tendency to compound until you are left with a second-rate product or package. You want to end up with the quality and value you initially imagined—and you can if you're a samurai about the details.

If you can't draw and "don't know a thing about design," you can simply borrow from the best. I don't mean infringing on another product's trade dress! I mean what I did when I went to drugstores and studied cosmetics packaging in order to get ideas for merchandising the D-Fuzz-It®. As consumers, we all know more about design than we think we do.

Pay attention to what attracts you in ads, in the grocery store, at the drugstore, everywhere. What colors catch your eye? What's in style but is classic enough to outlast fashion? What kind of type grabs you and gets its message across? Whenever we prepare to launch a new product, the people in my product development lab go out and do exactly this kind of research.

> *People want economy, and they'll pay any price to get it.*
> **LEE IACOCCA**

When you see something clever, make a mental note. As we've already discussed, a great deal of inventing is building on what's come before, not reinventing the wheel. Study what works and, as TV chef Emeril Lagasse says, "Kick it up a notch."

## MAKING SURE THE PRICE IS RIGHT

Like your product's name and package, its price is also a key factor in making a positive first impression.

You might think that a product's price is based solely on what it costs the manufacturer to make, distribute and market. But other factors come into play. While I believe in focusing less on what the market will bear and more on making a fair profit and delivering honest value, there are other strategies.

We've talked about the fairly standard 4-to-1 markup, and how a company's low or high overhead can affect that. But industry standards vary. Cosmetics often retail at ten times their cost due in large part to their massive advertising budgets. And products are sometimes priced high just to give the illusion of greater quality. It's not my practice, but it happens all the time.

The two most common strategies are to price low, in order to capture market share, or price high, to convey exceptional quality. If you price low, you hope your reduced per unit profits will be offset by increased sales— and that your buyers will remain loyal if you subsequently increase your price. If you price high, your initial sales may be smaller, but they may be made to more influential buyers—and if you subsequently drop your price, you'll be perceived as offering a great deal.

Think about how you make buying decisions. If you're like me you sometimes go for particular brands no matter what their price, and at other times buy whatever brand is on sale or priced the lowest. You weigh price against value. If you are convinced that a particular laundry soap makes your whites whiter, your brights brighter and smells like springtime, you'll probably be willing to buy it over and over again even if it costs a bit more. But if you think any old laundry soap will do, you'll buy the cheapest one. When you're selling a product, if you can't convince consumers that the value you offer is worth a price that allows you to make a profit, you're out of business.

Your product and market research should have given you a clear idea of pricing standards in your field. You might also have polled people on how much they would be willing to pay for the product they were testing. Polling is easier than ever these days with the many online polling and survey tools available.

As noted above, while SKYY® is a premium vodka, we can sell it for less than the other premium brands because we manufacture domestically. We see and have positioned Vermeer as an affordable indulgence—an "everyday luxury" like champagne or a good wine, with a price comparable to that of Baileys® Irish Cream.

As usual, solid research is essential in determining a price. Study and know your market and your consumer. Understand your product's essential value and work to manufacture and deliver that value in a way that affords you an honest profit.

## WHAT'S THE BUZZ? SPREAD-THE-WORD DISTRIBUTION AND MARKETING

We've seen that distributing SKYY® posed a real challenge. Unless you license your invention, or sell and distribute it yourself, as I did with the D-Fuzz-It®, obtaining good distribution will be one of your challenges as well.

Back when I created SKYY®, there was no Internet. Well, there was an Internet but no one outside the military and academia knew about it. We had no Facebook, chat rooms, blogs, Amazon reviews, or any other way to easily and cheaply get thousands of potential customers talking about SKYY® and build demand. I'll talk about Internet marketing in the next section, but for now here's a look at our old-fashioned methods that worked smashingly well. And pay attention, because these techniques are still extremely valid today.

You'll recall that our initial SKYY® distributor was a small local imported-beer distributor who agreed to add a case or two of SKYY® to his truck. We simply couldn't get anyone else to take us on. The San Francisco Bay Area was our initial test market and between that smallish market and our lack of a track record, the big distributors we approached turned us away with, "Why should we have our sales force promote you when we have Absolut?"

Our distributor didn't have a sales force per se, so Dave Stoop and I made sales and faxed the orders in to the guy with the truck. As we've seen, my employees and I also worked nonstop to build our presence. As people heard our name, saw us at events, and read about SKYY® and congeners in newspapers, our distributor began to get calls and orders.

Buoyed by our good results, we moved to statewide distribution and this time hooked up with a wine distributor. By now we could photocopy articles about SKYY® that had appeared in the press and give our sales reps this additional ammunition for sales calls.

You can't depend on distributors to do it all for you. Please read that sentence again; it's that important. They won't stick with a slow-moving product no matter how well established you are. Distributors sell products that sell, and their sales forces will rally behind products that sell. YOU make that happen. For SKYY®, that meant cultivating word of mouth, being visible at events, and earning publicity with the SKYY® story. (We didn't begin advertising until we were already a success.)

Make your customers de facto sales reps, or as Guy Kawasaki might say, evangelists. Bartenders played that role for us. When we convinced them of SKYY®'s value, they spread the word to their customers, who then bought SKYY® at their local liquor stores and called for it by name at other bars and restaurants.

When we made the switch to cobalt blue, our sales got quite a boost. When we went to the annual Wine and Spirits Wholesalers of America trade show in New Orleans that year, distributors approached us, wanting to work with us on national distribution because they had heard how well we were doing.

When it came time to distribute SKYY® in Europe, we faced distribution issues all over again. I didn't want to set up remote branch offices and hire and manage our own people abroad. The solution lay in the forming of strategic alliances. For instance, Campari International sold well throughout Europe and Asia, and had an in-place infrastructure and distribution network. We made a deal for Campari to represent

SKYY® overseas and we became their exclusive U.S. importer. In a short time, Campari found themselves selling twice as much SKYY® as they'd forecasted in Italy—not traditionally a vodka-drinking country. Salute!

And as mentioned earlier, the Campari deal worked out so well that when we were ready to sell SKYY® they were ready to buy.

Snapple®'s David and Goliath story bears some resemblance to SKYY®'s and is worth mentioning in this context. Founded by three entrepreneurs from Brooklyn, Snapple® developed a solid base in New York City health food stores and then gradually expanded their product line and distribution into supermarkets and delicatessens.

In order to implement their idea for a preservative-free, real-brewed ice tea, they innovated a "hot fill" bottling process similar to home canning. This highly successful tea attracted large distributors to Snapple®.

The nonalcoholic carbonated and noncarbonated drink business is dominated by a few giants. In 1994, Coke and Pepsi held 72% of the entire market. Superpower Pepsi partnered with Lipton® Tea to compete with Snapple® and create a bottled tea, but, as is often the case with gigantic companies, it took them several years to do so. (Unencumbered by plodding, bureaucratic research, development and decision-making processes, small entrepreneurial outfits can often out-pace larger, established organizations.) But when Pepsi-Lipton® did fight back, they fought hard, questioning Snapple®'s brewing process and using the full weight of their distribution network to launch their Lipton® Original everywhere. Snapple® beefed up their advertising but also benefited greatly by having been first to market with their tea. Plus, Snapple®'s niche—natural "New Age" beverages—became a growing market trend. Finally, and also like SKYY®, Snapple® brought top industry professionals into their operation, crafted exciting consumer advertising, and launched its line in Europe, all while staying true to their initial quality and image. (Thomas 1995, pp. 290-97) They're still a major brand in 2013, owned by Dr. Pepper Snapple® Group. But let's get back to the basics.

There are an increasing number of ways to get your product to its consumer, and as usual, your imagination, creativity, and enthusiasm are key to making any of them work. Routes include:

- *Stores*

- *The Internet: online retail*

- *The Internet: promotion of any other sales channel*

- *Catalogs*

- *Infomercials*

- *Direct Mail*

- *Use As a Promo Item*

Let's look at a few of these options. You may be surprised to learn that you can pitch your product to huge retail outlets like Wal-Mart. Find out when and how they see new products and make your case. (See appendix for contact information.) If I were bringing my SKYY® Timer in for consideration, I'd do a little something extra like bring in a dozen printed with "Wal-Mart Time" instead of "SKYY® Timer." I'd hand one out to everyone I could, knowing that using the device is the best way to discover its worth.

Look for small mail-order catalogs that handle of similar gadgets and make a pitch to them. Maybe you've got something The Sharper Image® or Hammacher Schlemmer® would be interested in. Both of these retail and catalog outfits regularly look at new inventions and products. In the past, Hammacher Schlemmer® even ran a *Search for Invention* contest that rewarded inventors of patented products that had not yet reached the marketplace. (See appendix for details.)

I might consider doing an infomercial to sell my microfiber pillow. It's not a bad idea. Many products have been known to move on into established retail markets after succeeding in the world of infomercials. Some infomercial production companies will even look at a product in the design stage, and if they like it, handle manufacturing.

Another avenue I considered for my SKYY® Timer was offering it to another company for use as a promotional item for them. David Pressman cites the famous example of eight-year-old Abbey Mae Fleck who invented a plastic device for hanging bacon in a microwave so that the grease dripped away while it cooked. She couldn't get any manufacturers of microwave accessories interested and so she had the very bright idea of approaching a bacon company. They put a discount coupon for her product on their packages and it was a huge success. (Pressman 1997, pp. 11, 13) Like SKYY®, almost every kind of company uses promotional items that can be emblazoned with their name and either increase their sales or simply keep their name in the public's eye.

No matter what distribution channels you pursue, remember that distributing is a business and, like all businesses, needs to be profitable in order to survive. Even in this age of do-it-yourself sales and marketing on Amazon and eBay, the distributor model is still alive and well. After all, do you really want your garage or living room to become your warehouse, and do you really want to pack and ship all those orders yourself? The right distributor can help your company and your sales grow, but they don't exist solely for your benefit. So show them what's in it for them. Persuade them that your product will generate inquiries and sales. Convince them that you will promote the product and then do it.

## PUBLICITY, PROMOTION AND ADVERTISING

I'm told that it is rare for an inventor, who often has a science or engineering background as I do, to also be interested in marketing, which I am. I actually find the two areas complementary. Successful inventing is every bit as creative as good marketing, and it pays to approach marketing logically.

Many inventors have also been hands-on marketers. Robert Augustus Chesebrough, the inventor of Vaseline®, was one. I scootered around San Francisco, visiting liquor stores with SKYY®, and he traveled around upper New York State in a horse and buggy, giving jars of Vaseline® to anyone who would take it. His version of my daily SKYY® martini was a spoonful of Vaseline® each and every day. He claimed he lived to age ninety-six because of his daily dose, and I hope my ritual does the same for me!

While it's certainly possible to stay in your lab or workroom and hire people to package and sell your inventions, I find marketing exciting and fun. No one understands my inventions better than I do. But if marketing is not of interest to you, sales and marketing associates can be people you hire to be part of your company, outside experts your company contracts with or a division of the manufacturing firm you license. Your company can also concentrate on sales and marketing while subcontracting the manufacturing. The choice you make depends on your interests and skills.

Dave Stoop was a kid studying at San Francisco State and working as a caterer when he heard about SKYY®. He thought it was a great idea and approached me about part-time work. I talked him into working full-time as my first salesperson, and he soon became known around San Francisco as Mr. SKYY®.

In our office, four people had to fight for the use of the three phone lines but Dave was rarely there; San Francisco was his office. He visited liquor stores by day and restaurants by night, where he'd drink one cappuccino after another while pouring taste tests for bartenders and restaurateurs.

We did our taste tests against the top-selling premium brands— Absolut, Stolichnya® and Finlandia®. We nearly always won. This one-to-one selling was part of our low-budget strategy for building a market presence.

Because our bottle was so attractive and so different from any other, we were able to do striking window displays in stores. The way light hits the bottle is just spectacular, so merchants were happy to have our displays up for months on end.

When I was twelve and growing up in Brooklyn, my best friend Harvey and I started a business, HarMor Photography. Basically we took pictures on spec. If the neighbors said they didn't want to have their picture taken, we said, "Smile!" and took the picture anyway. When we showed them a print, they could rarely resist buying a copy. When a restaurant, store or bar resisted selling SKYY®, we persevered, giving them a taste test, creating an attractive display or offering them a risk-free investment. Nine times out of ten, when they saw the results, we were in business.

Aside from SKYY® itself, we had a brochure I'd written, "Whyy SKYY®?" that laid out the science and innovation behind the brand, plus T-shirts and key chains with our logo. Today we'd also have a website, Facebook page, the works. We left those promo items everywhere we went: phone booths, cabs, even restrooms. Through the years, SKYY® became known for unusual, useful giveaways. We had SKYY® wristwatches made in the style of some of the most popular brands. I once asked the fellow sitting next to me on a New York to London flight for the time. He looked at his SKYY® watch. I asked who gave it to him and it turned out to have been my nephew who was marketing SKYY® in the Hamptons. (We'd targeted that upscale Long Island enclave when we brought SKYY® out East.)

We always tried to use promo pieces that offered some value to the customer—nothing intricate or expensive, just fun, handy, branded items that people will keep and use. Vision is an interest of mine so I put a chart that tests for color blindness on the back of our brochure. If you can read the letters S-K-Y-Y, you have good color vision. People love to test themselves with such things and it's a fun thing to show a friend— especially one who makes weird color choices!

We made SKYY® martini atomizers (vermouth spray) and did a co-promotion with a gourmet olive company to create SKYY® boxes filled with a metal shaker (with a SKYY® logo, of course), two glasses, an atomizer and a jar of olives.

We also produced something called SKYY® Eyes, strips of plastic with tiny pinholes that, when held up to the eyes, bring blurred images into focus (they also function as swizzle sticks). I was sitting at home one day, listening to a local radio station. The talk-show host mentioned that he'd forgotten his glasses and was having a hard time reading his materials. I got on my scooter, rode to the station across town, and left a pair of SKYY® Eyes and my business card with the receptionist. The talk-show host got a big kick out of the glasses—and gave SKYY® a nice plug.

Our distribution widened and our sales skyrocketed when newspapers, magazines and television began telling our story. No amount of advertising could have the impact of a story in *USA Today* or a five-minute interview on CNBC. Lots of these media outlets were skeptical about our claims. They grilled me and went out and conducted their own taste and morning-after tests. We passed with flying colors, and I had the science to back me up. We can't promise "purity" or guarantee "no hangovers," but people who tried SKYY® were pleased with their results, and these news stories got more people to check us out. Today, the power of social media sites like Facebook and Twitter could magnify such results to an incalculable degree.

> *Advertising in the final analysis should be news. If it is not news, it is worthless.*
>
> **ADOLPH S. OCHS, PUBLISHER AND EDITOR**

Our experience with the press is another instance of how valuable having a legitimate story to tell can be. Not every new product is newsworthy and the media won't gratuitously plug products. These days the Internet makes press releases really easy to submit. Consequently, it seems that every company makes a release every time the CEO sneezes so the media is rather flooded with them. Fortunately, this also means that reporters and blog writers (there are more of them than ever) are always looking for truly interesting material. So if your product or invention is "fit to print," if it can make a provocative claim like SKYY®, if it's the first of its kind like the Quad, or if there is a significant charitable aspect like my inexpensive plastic glasses, bring it to the media's attention with a press release. They also look good posted to your website, and they might impress an investor.

As Bob Coleman and Deborah Neville point out, in 1991, Ben & Jerry's made it onto the *Wall Street Journal*'s front page and the cover of *Inc.* magazine not because of Ben & Jerry's ice cream but because of Ben and Jerry. Having a new ice cream, even one with funnily named flavors, isn't a story, but being "two counter-culture guys... trying to build a big business without betraying their principles" is. The *Wall Street Journal*'s price for a full-page ad in the same paper in which the Ben & Jerry's story ran was

$105,352. Who can afford to buy that kind of publicity? (Coleman and Neville 1993, pp. 268-69)

For many years, Racing Strollers, Inc.'s Baby Jogger® relied primarily on word-of-mouth and customer usage promotion, taking out only modest ads in *Runner's World* and *Parents*. But the uniqueness of the product has also made it newsworthy, earning stories in publications including the *Wall Street Journal, Washington Post, USA Today*, and *The New York Times*. (Thomas 1995, p. 178) Nowadays, it's all over the Internet as well, because of the many stores that sell it.

At SKYY® we took full advantage of all the publicity that came our way, from *Newsweek* to the supermarket tabloid *Star*. The latter ran an item trumpeting, "the new Hollywood fad is a brand of vodka, which is supposed to be hangover-free. JACK NICHOLSON loves the stuff and has it delivered to his house." If SKYY® hadn't been delivered to his house before, it soon was because we hastily sent him a case—as well as sending copies of the blurb to influential bars and restaurants. We distributed copies of all the articles that were written about us to our distributors and customers—spread the news.

SKYY® didn't begin advertising until we were already successful. We didn't use advertising to build the brand; we used it to enhance the brand after free publicity, word of mouth and promotions had already put us on a roll.

When we did begin advertising, we were conservative in some ways, innovative in others. We got the most for our money by purchasing one-third page vertical ads because an ad the full height of a magazine but just one column wide will be placed next to editorial rather than other ads. We advertised in the kind of magazines we believed had "influential" readers, like *Architectural Digest, Gourmet* and *Wired*. We even ran in *Popular Science* because I believed that the kind of people who read a science magazine would appreciate the science behind SKYY®—and tell their friends. We also broke ground by advertising early on in gay publications, such as the *Advocate* and *Out*. As SKYY® grew, we moved into full-page advertising.

Events were also key to SKYY®'s early success. We showed up at every event we heard about—society parties, charity events, symphony galas, fund-raising benefits. We donated cases of SKYY®, and walked around pouring people martinis. Who could refuse? We made up some martini glasses with our logo on them and women in evening gowns fought over them.

People who regularly attended such events saw SKYY® and became curious about it. They may also have read the brochure we put in their gift bag or noticed that they didn't get the usual morning-after headaches. In any event, they started calling for SKYY® at bars and restaurants. They spread the word for us.

We wanted to get SKYY® into the hands of influential trendsetters and opinion shapers. We knew that if we got it into their hands once, they'd reach for it themselves the next time. Marketing professionals routinely target their efforts at specific demographics, but I'm talking about something more subtle. Think not only about your end user but also about the people who influence your end user. Who are the trendsetters and opinion shapers in your product area? How do you reach them? On the Internet, these trendsetters write blogs, send out Twitter tweets, have well-known Facebook pages, and write articles for industry journals, websites, and blogs. Those who follow all this will get your message through them.

This process of influencing various tiers of buyers is sometimes referred to as getting imitators to follow innovators. Business school professor and corporate consultant Robert J. Thomas describes the way highly innovative products gain acceptance. "Innovators, a small proportion of the total potential market, are very eager to buy the new product, and do so. The hope is that imitators will soon follow... and boost the volume of sales." (Thomas 1995, p. 8) SKYY®'s acceptance by innovators, the trendsetters and opinion shapers we initially targeted, fostered a much wider level of consumption

In 1916, Nathan Handwerker promoted his new frankfurters by giving doctors at the nearby Coney Island Hospital free franks—if they ate them at his stand while wearing their white coats and stethoscopes. He hoped the public's respect for doctors would rub off on his product and prove that Nathan's Franks were healthy and high quality. (Panati 1987, p. 397)

Who is your target audience? Who do they respect? Who and what influences their buying habits? What websites and blogs to they follow? It's your business to know.

Agencies and consultants use elaborate research to direct and place your ads, promotions and online posts. I think we did a pretty good job on our own and you can assemble much of the same kind of information yourself. If it gets to be too much trying to find all the online resources you should pursue, there are firms and software that can help you.

If you're trying to determine ideal target regions for launching your product, you can obtain a wealth of information on population through the Census Report and on government Websites (for example: demographia. com). In considering the importation of a new line of scooters, we used U.S. Department of Transportation information to learn the penetration of motor scooter sales and Census Bureau information to locate regions with the highest percentage of the target audience we identified (college students and young working adults). This information was free on the Internet.

Before deciding where to place advertising, check the circulation audits of the publications you are considering and ask website administrators for their demographic stats. Many publications can also provide you with general studies of national buying habits by age, gender, occupation, etc., through MRI surveys (named after the company that runs these surveys, Mediamark Research and Intelligence.) Many if not all online advertising programs target ads based upon demographic data, known user profiles, and keyword searches, all in an effort to place relevant ads in front of the correct audience.

Trade journals and company websites can tell you what your competition is doing. Often sales figures, profits and areas of distribution are listed in easy to interpret graphs and charts.

San Francisco's Castro District drinkers understood SKYY®'s value and embraced its style from the very beginning. And the gay community's influence extends far beyond any neighborhood, affecting popular culture on a variety of significant levels, from fashion and consumer goods to music, movies and every aspect of the entertainment arts. We nurtured this relationship by advertising in gay publications and sponsoring events.

Because I love film and also because the film community wields considerable power to create trends and influence tastes, we cultivated a presence in the independent film world. In addition to sponsoring events at Bay Area film festivals, we sponsored parties at film festivals in Nantucket, Newport, Cannes and Chicago. We went narrow and deep into this market, rather than going wide and shallow into many. We knew that penetrating one or two targeted markets would have a domino effect on other markets.

## USING THE INTERNET TO CREATE BUZZ

When we began marketing SKYY®, the Internet and all its myriad marketing opportunities did not exist as it does now. For the new inventor in the second decade of the 21st Century and beyond, the Internet is a spectacular way to build buzz and augment your more traditional marketing efforts. The excitement you create can carry far beyond your local area through venues like Facebook, YouTube, and blogs.

I caution you to not rely solely on the Internet to promote your product. These days it's easy to get so wrapped up in all the online marketing opportunities that you lose track of the basics. But online and offline marketing need to function cooperatively. After all, you can't drink a SKYY® martini online. If I had all these Internet tools back when we were starting SKYY®, I would still have gone around town delivering cases to skeptical barkeepers. There is no substitute for that personal contact. The Web is great for spreading excitement by word of mouth, but at some point you need to put a good product into people's hands so they can discover that they love it. Then they'll start talking about it in the real world and online.

This section is not going to turn you into an ace online marketer. Online marketing is very complex and people make entire careers out of it. But I do hope to give you some ideas about how to promote your new product and get people talking about it. Much of this stuff is still very new, and the experts themselves often can't agree on how to use it. My organization uses some but not all of these techniques, but we're working on it.

Each of the topics in this section represents a whole field of study in its own right. There are many self-help books, websites, blogs, research papers, and opinion pieces online that give you all you need and more. I've listed some of those in the Appendix. If in the end it all proves too much, find someone who knows what they're doing, give them a piece of the pie, and let them manage online marketing for you. Every brand I manage has its own marketing team, and paying Internet people to do Internet stuff just makes sense.

## YOUR WEBSITE

Every company and product needs its own well-designed and well-written website as an online base of operations. Your core messaging, content, product images, press releases, showcase of partner companies, videos, and other public-facing stuff will live there. Every time you do something with Facebook, Twitter, or YouTube it should link back to your home base. Every promotion should be tied to matching online content. Announce promotional events on your site beforehand and show the results afterward. Imagine the effect of photos or videos of happy beautiful people dancing and having a good time and clamoring for more of your product. OK, if your product is a new type of orthopaedic splint maybe they won't be dancing but you get the idea.

Websites are cheap to create, but tricky to do right. You can program one yourself, or use one of many low-cost platforms like WordPress or SquareSpace. There are thousands of local and online web development services you could use. But you have to get the content and design right. As with your product's name, packaging, label, color, scent, taste, and so forth, your website must be a thorough reflection of your brand, tell its story clearly and briefly, build trust, and convince people of its value. If it fails in any of these you need to get some qualified help.

A website needs pertinent content that is updated regularly. Turn your site into an online attraction by publishing material that will make people want to go there again and again. On the Blue Angel site we have recipes for our signature Blue Angel Martini (BAM), BlueBAM, CranBAM and Angelrita. Videos of promotional parties and write-ups on the local bar scene would be smart additions (note to self: contact marketing team.) On the SooFoo™ site we have an introductory video, tips on healthy living and recipes in addition to the usual "About Us" and "How to Buy" information. Find out what your target market is interested in, and then illustrate how your product supports those interests.

### EBAY, AMAZON, AND OTHER SELL-IT-YOURSELF SITES

There are loads of sites where you can manage your own online storefront, and they are great for the right product and the right market. If you're going after doctors or the government, forget it, but consumer products could do well. Keep your expectations realistic because these sites typically don't offer the branded marketing, focused promotion, and trust-building environment you need to build buzz around a brand new product. You should rely primarily on your own website and other efforts, and look at these sites as utilities for secure checkout and sources for a large pool of potential buyers.

### SEARCH ENGINE OPTIMIZATION (SEO)

Chances are that as you read this, someone is searching online, looking for something just like your invention. They are trying to solve a problem but they don't know about you or your product so they "Google" on a variety of words and terms, hoping to hit on something. When they get their list of ten-billion search results they are more than likely to click on only the top two or three. Search engine optimization, or SEO, is the art and science of tweaking your website content, keywords and code for a better ranking by search engines. People make entire careers out of SEO. If you're really serious about selling online, take an afternoon to learn SEO basics from one of the many websites and blogs out there. Some top SEO activities include:

- *Adding keywords frequently and logically to your website copy. This one is big.*

- *Adding accurate and descriptive "meta tags" to your page code. Work with your Webmaster on this.*

- *Linking to as many other pertinent pages as you legitimately can.*

- *Using a web service or platform that creates meaningful descriptive URLs (web addresses) that use actual words rather than gobbledygook strings of digits and letters.*

- *Adding a "robots.txt" file that tells search engines which of your pages they should and should not list.*

- *Submitting your site to the search engines.*

## ANALYTICS

Analytics tools like Google Analytics (free for the basic package) and the industry-leading Omniture (pricey for smaller companies) will track tons of different metrics. You can calculate the effectiveness of every SEO tweak, promotion, campaign, product announcement, Facebook post, change in marketing copy, and practically anything else you do online. The idea is to analyze what happens, build on winning strategies, and fix the losing strategies. You can tell for instance, whether it's your blog or your online coupon that is generating all those sales on your *eBay* store. Analytics, along with SEO, is one of the biggest disciplines within e-commerce and deserves its own book. Check the Appendix for a couple recommendations.

## PAID SEARCH ENGINE ADS

You can pay for ads that the search engines display on the page of search results. You specify the keywords or phrases that should trigger your ad to appear, and typically pay according to the value the search engine places on those keywords or phrases. If your budget allows, try them for a month or two and see how they do. There is a whole world of other types of online advertising, which you may want to try.

## BLOGS

A Web log or "blog" is a website where you regularly add new material. Highly interested customers often follow blogs, contribute to the "comments" section, and attract other readers. Blogs are great if you have promotions, product releases, customer stories, events, and new uses for your product, or anything else that warrants regular updates. You should also post pertinent information (like articles on related topics) that is not about the product itself but is important to your target market. Multiply the effect of your blog (and other online efforts) by preparing a brief pitch and contacting other bloggers who are subject matter experts (SMEs) in your field. Offer to demo your new gizmo. Bloggers are always looking for new material and one or two might just blog about you. If they provide links to your sites it can dramatically increase visits to your website, blog, Facebook, etc., so prepare in advance by posting good solid content.

## VIDEO

People love video. Chances are good that if you put a video product demo on your home page, people will watch it, particularly if it is short—say thirty to sixty seconds. Companies large and small are using video, and they're making it do double or triple duty by posting it in multiple places: home pages, YouTube, blogs, partner sites, and so forth. Your video does not need to be expensive. All you need to do is tell your story honestly, preferably in an offbeat or humorous way.

One of my favorites is the "Will it Blend" series from Utah-based blender manufacturer Blendtec. Back in 2006, Blendtec VP of Marketing George Wright happened to see founder and president Tom Dickson testing one of his new blenders by blending up a piece of 2x2 lumber.[1] George decided (rightly) that this would make great marketing material. They taped Tom blending up a hardwood rake handle in the company break room. They added some opening titles and game show-style music. It exploded when it hit YouTube and became one of the most successful viral marketing campaigns ever. Check it out on YouTube at http://www.youtube.com/watch?v=aM94aorYVS4. Dozens more Will it Blend videos followed, where Tom nonchalantly blended such unusual items as glass marbles, cans of soda (including the can), and the occasional iPhone.

You can make some remarkably effective videos yourself on a very low budget. Borrow a video camera if you need to, and someone who knows how to use it. Don't think you have to hire an expensive video production team and actors. Watch other videos for inspiration, try to be entertaining, and don't put on pretenses (unless pretense is part of your shtick).

Use your videos to demonstrate the value of the product, show people having fun using it, illustrate how to use it, and show how to get the most out of it. It is better to create several short videos than one really big one. Our SooFoo™ site has a video front and center with commentators explaining recipes and extolling the product's versatility.

> • SPAM laws say that promotional email can only be legitimately (or legally) sent out to people who have actively asked you to send them email, or "opted in". If you get enough SPAM complaints you can easily get blacklisted and your email provider could block you from sending.

## EMAIL

Be cautious of email. Email is great for promoting to existing customers and keeping them interested, but it's no good for attracting new customers. That's because the SPAM laws say that promotional email can only be legitimately (or legally) sent out to people who have actively asked you to send them email, or "opted in". A good email list is important in generating repeat sales and promoting future products. Add a "Sign up for Email" link to all your promotions and every page of your site. Lots of people will want email about events, new products, promotions, product updates, and so forth. Just be careful; never buy or rent an email list from a third party even if they claim it has great qualifications, and don't email to your own list unless the people on it have specifically opted in. If you get enough

SPAM complaints you can easily get blacklisted and your email provider could block you from sending. Most customer service emails are allowed under SPAM laws if they are one-on-one communications with an existing customer or someone who has contacted you. If you want to send bulk promotional email, sign up with a tried-and-true email service provider like Constant Contact, MailChimp, Bronto, or Cheetahmail and follow their guidelines.

> *In the groundswell, relationships are everything. The way people connect with each other—the community that is created—determines how the power shifts.*
> **CHARLENE LI AND JOSH BERNOFF,** *GROUNDSWELL* **(P. 18)**

## QR CODES

A QR code is similar to a barcode but looks like a jumbled-up checkerboard. It can store information like phone numbers, website addresses, product names and much more. Many mobile phones and other devices can read QR codes. Marketers have been using them like mad lately, because a shopper standing in a store aisle can scan them to open the product's website, view a video, get a discount, compare prices, and read online reviews. Put a QR code on every product package, in every print ad, on the side of your car, and on every promotional item so an intrigued observer can pop on over to your site or get a discount code at their moment of greatest interest. We put a QR code on the back of some Blue Angel bar coasters so patrons would have immediate access to "where to buy it" information on our website. I'd have put a QR code on the SKYY® timer if they existed at the time.

## SOURCE CODES OR COUPON CODES

On their websites, online retailers often provide a little box where the customer can type a source code or coupon code. Each code represents a discount or special offer of some type, and is activated during checkout.

Put a different source code on every ad or campaign you run, and you'll know for sure which one worked best. Put an online coupon on a partner's website and assign it a unique source code for a discount. Or offer two-for-one for someone who watches your YouTube video. It's all part of getting people to try the product and encourage their friends to try it.

## SOCIAL MEDIA

In their 2008 book, *Groundswell*, Charlene Li and Josh Bernoff of Forrester Research explain how social media or social computing is turning marketing on its head. This new movement is "A social trend in which people use technologies to get the things they need from each other, rather than from traditional institutions like corporations."[2]

It used to be that the only voice anyone ever heard was the marketer's, because only marketers could afford TV ads, newspaper ads, product placements, and other mass communications. Customer feedback was limited to local word of mouth, comments to retail personnel, and the occasional letter.

That has all changed in the last five to ten years, starting with online customer reviews and proceeding through fully interactive sites like Facebook. The marketer can no longer dictate the message—the message is now part of a larger conversation between the marketer and the community of hundreds, thousands, or even millions of other like-minded netizens. They will talk about your product online, post compliments and gripes, and hopefully tell each other how much they liked it and where to buy it. The things they write may have more influence than anything you say or do, because consumers always trust other consumers more than they trust marketers.

Though scary sounding at first, this is actually excellent news for the new inventor. Those institutions that have lost control of their audience may be your competition, and you can become the one to whom the people turn "to get the things they need." It is possible to reach a broad market very inexpensively, though it will take time and effort. Every time someone "Likes" you on Facebook or recommends your product in a discussion forum, it's an opportunity for your website URL to be duplicated and forwarded again and again. It can work its way into places you could never reach otherwise. Services and software like HootSuite and TweetDeck help you track and manage what people are saying about you on social media, which can significantly decrease the time you spend sorting through it all. By the time you read this, the social media tools may have changed but I'll bet the core techniques I describe will remain very similar.

## DISCUSSION BOARDS

There are online discussion boards for every topic under the sun. Hobbies, health care, careers, and specific products—you name it and there's a discussion board for it. Folks wanting to learn about something often go to discussion boards because the participants talk about their personal experiences, new products, how-to, and related topics. Product recommendations (and warnings) by actual users abound. Product vendors often participate, but they need to be careful; most boards will kick you out if your posts are too self-serving. Instead, listen to the conversation, offer advice as a subject matter expert, subtly mention your product, and see what people say. If anyone wants to know more, invite them to a conversation offline or via email. A good reputation in the right discussion board can alert your target market and generate buzz. Think in terms of becoming recognized as a subject matter expert.

## FACEBOOK

As I write this, Facebook is still The Big One. Everyone has been talking about Facebook, but the only agreement is that each marketer has to tailor its own Facebook presence to suit itself. Facebook does offer some merchandising features, and a number of third parties provide retail applications that allow you to sell your products through Facebook. My organization has not used those because we prefer to link from Facebook to our other sites. As with the sell-it-yourself sites, I suspect there is greater benefit to be had from relying primarily on your own custom website, at least until sales start to take off. My advice is to use Facebook to create a dialog between you and your target market and to encourage your fans to spread the word. Some things to post on Facebook include:

- *New product announcements*
- *Promotion announcements, coupon codes, campaign messages*
- *Customer service announcements*
- *New photos or videos*
- *Invitations to online or offline events*
- *Invitations to take part in polls, surveys, contests*
- *Customer comments, stories, photos, videos*

We get folks involved with the SooFoo™ Facebook page by running contests—"Like" us and win a SooFoo™ cooker—and by encouraging our fans to submit their own SooFoo™ recipes. We've got about 4,000 Likes so far, which I'm told is pretty good.

Facebook does have rules about commerce on their site, so make sure you understand them thoroughly before you lay your plans. Also, plan to either use one of the automated social media management tools, or spend a few hours a week composing and managing your updates and responding to inquiries.

## YOUTUBE

Google is the world's most popular search engine. No surprise there. YouTube is the world's second most popular search engine,[3] with people using it much like they use Google. YouTube is owned by Google, and videos on YouTube often show up very high in Google search results. If you put even a simple video on YouTube, it significantly boosts the chances of your product showing up in Google searches. This means YouTube may provide someone their first-ever exposure to your product.

Where does the first-time martini maker go when they want to mix their own at home? YouTube or Google, to find an instructional video. We've posted several videos about mixing Blue Angel Martinis, and several of our fans have too. I'd like to make one showing a bunch of bar patrons saying how good a BAM is. This all increases the chances of Blue Angel Vodka showing up when someone searches Google for "martini", "cocktail", or "vodka".

Viewer comments are an integral part of the YouTube experience. You post a video, and then if you are lucky the viewers will comment favorably about your product. YouTube and Google index all their entries, so the more they talk the more likely your product will show up in other searches.

Some people are so enraptured with a product they become brand advocates (or evangelists—see Kawasaki page ---) and make their own YouTube videos. These advocates really get into this, reviewing products and showing them in use. Each enthusiast's video is a commercial for your product. If you can start a conversation with your brand advocates and keep them happy, you have a potential gold mine because each of those advocates will influence people you never hear from yourself.

## TWITTER

What can you say in 140 characters? In the case of Twitter, I think it's not the value of any one particular "tweet", but the value of everything you say added up. You'll get the most out of Twitter (and other social media platforms) if you generate a large following. I think Twitter is most useful for…

- *New product announcements*

- *Promotion announcements, coupon codes, campaign messages*

- *Invitations to online or offline events*

- *Customer service announcements*

Use Twitter's hashtag feature to tag the keywords you want to emphasize, and your message will show up more readily when people search on those words.

## GOOGLE+

Most of the same rules apply to Google+ as they do to other social networks. At the time I write this, Google+ still trails Facebook by a wide margin, but it's worth watching because of the Google name and because of the public's growing interest. Google+ has a number of sharing capabilities, including Streams, Circles, and Hangouts, which are too numerous to go into here.

## PINTEREST

Pinterest lets you share photos in a social context. If you have a product that lends itself to being shown visually, then do so. Show your product in use, and encourage your early adopters to pin photos of them using it. Explain the context of the images in captions. Be the subject matter expert. Pinterest is encouraging business use, with robust profiles, links, the ability to post your promotions, optimization for mobile devices, traffic generation tools, community tools, and a bunch more.

## LINKEDIN

LinkedIn is the de-facto online network for businesses and professionals. If your invention is primarily for business use, then LinkedIn is a great place to reach those in your target industry. Build your network, position yourself as a subject matter expert, and don't sell too hard. Explore the LinkedIn Groups discussion boards. You'll find professionals interested in all kinds of targeted subject areas. If you're promoting an office product like Zip Notes™, participate in groups for office managers. A nurses' group would be right if I were promoting the Safetyglide™ needle protector. LinkedIn also offers plenty of opportunity to link to your site, your blog, Facebook, YouTube and other online resources.

## USER-GENERATED CONTENT

Many companies encourage their community of users to create and submit their own content to the company website: product reviews, responses to surveys and polls, videos, photos, user stories, and more. We actively campaign to get SooFoo™ customers to send us recipes. This is a great way for your best customers to become your advocates, because would-be buyers trust other customers more than they trust a marketer, and participation like this encourages still more participation. Of course, if you have problems with your product you could end up with a bunch of negative reviews and online "flames" but that is the risk we all take in this day of interactive marketing. Make user-generated content do double duty by re-posting it on Facebook, YouTube and other appropriate venues.

## PREPARING FOR BAD NEWS

Keep in mind that as good as the Web is at spreading positive news about a product people love, it is even better at spreading bad news about a product that fails, or a company that lets its customers down. Negative comments and reviews can plague even established manufacturers, and if your product disappoints someone badly enough it can be all over blogs, Facebook and Twitter before you know it.

You are likely to receive bad comments somewhere along the line. Some will be from your competitors trying to tarnish your reputation. Some will likely be legitimate. Prepare in advance by making your product as good as it can be, by being honest about what it can do and what it can't, and by having a solid customer care policy in place where you support, replace or refund with no hassle. You can turn angry customers into staunch advocates this way.

## SOME PARTING COMMENTS

Some products are easier to build buzz around, and some are harder. It's up to you to find the right target market. Thousands of twenty-somethings may go nuts over premium vodka, whereas a target market of surgeons may be quietly pleased with a new tool for treating hernias.

As I mentioned in the blogging section, identify and contact the influential subject matter experts. They're the ones with lots of posts and lots of followers. Demo your product and get them to blog, post, tweet, review, or make a video about you. Their positive comments can influence a lot of readers and other SMEs.

Manage your online presence like a campaign, and make sure your message is consistent from one channel to the next—your website, email, print ads, brochures, YouTube, Facebook, and all the rest, online or off. Write the copy for your campaigns and your website, and then re-use all or bits of it in different channels. It should not all be identical, but elements like product descriptions, keywords, discount offers, and taglines should be the same. You want your customers to get a consistent message about your invention no matter where they are, and not end up thinking you are two different companies. Some variance is appropriate, like using different lead photos for different target markets.

Think before you post! One person's joke or clever comment is another person's insult. In October 2012, American Apparel used Twitter to announce their "Bored during the storm" sale,[4] promoting a discount to eastern U.S. states then being pounded by the disastrous tropical storm Sandy. Their insensitivity was rewarded with unflattering headlines, angry re-tweets, and calls for boycott. This kind of thing seems to happen all the time. With Twitter, Facebook, email, and other electronic media it is frighteningly easy for an ill-worded message to escape into the real world with just the slip of a finger and develop a life of its own.

And remember, your customers have the advantage of numbers! But don't let that scare you. Create a good product, market it honestly and most people will be kind to you.

Even without all the advantages of the Internet, we grew SKYY® from nothing, to a locally distributed phenomenon, to an internationally sold brand. Our small four-person office evolved into SKYY® Spirits LLC, a hundred-person plus company with a management team made up of the best people in the business. SKYY® became the second best-selling premium vodka in the U.S., the fastest growing brand, and a significant force in the alcohol beverage industry. To cap it all we sold it to one of the leading beverage concerns in the world. Not bad for an idea that sprang from a headache.

What I am perhaps most proud of with SKYY® is that it was a true example of the enduring power of inventive thinking coupled with an entrepreneurial spirit. As you've read, SKYY®'s success wasn't rocket science; it was based on good common sense and perseverance. As a broke kid with a nifty sweater comb and as a veteran inventor with a "crazy" idea for a new and improved vodka, life has shown me that if you develop a quality product, sell it at a fair price and shoot for an honest profit, you can prosper. The sky really is the limit.

## (ENDNOTES)

1   http://soni1220.wordpress.com/2011/02/20/viral-marketing-a-success-story-will-it-blend-that-is-the-question/ and http://www.socialens.com/wp-content/uploads/2009/04/20090127_case_blendtec11.pdf

2   Li, Charlene and Bernoff, Josh, "Groundswell" 2008, Forrester Research, Inc., Harvard Business Press, Boston. Page 9.

3   http://www.nytimes.com/2010/05/17/technology/17youtube.html?_r=0

4   http://mashable.com/2012/10/30/american-apparel-sandy/

    http://www.seomoz.org/beginners-guide-to-seo

    http://www.seomoz.org/ugc/four-seo-basics-that-helped-double-organic-traffic-and-sales-overnight

# Afterword
## The fundamental things still apply

Inventors don't retire, maybe because inventing doesn't really feel like work for many of us. So what's next for this inventor? Like Sam Farber and his Good Grips™ utensils, I think I have a few winners left in me. Al and the other folks at my lab can attest to the dozens of projects and patents we have in one stage of development or another.

One thing is certain, even in today's rapidly changing and ever evolving New Economy/Internet driven/high-tech world, there's still plenty of room for an old-fashioned good idea—one that solves a problem.

I think most inventors at one time or another dream of addressing problems on a vastly different scale than consumer convenience, timesaving or pleasure. I once was privileged to watch a patient regain his vision through a cataract removal procedure with my cryogenic device. Though that process has now been eclipsed by far more high-tech procedures, it remains my proudest achievement. As I write, I am working to organize and fund a free mobile clinic that will perform cataract removal procedures in India, a country I love to visit but also one of the world's poorest. We estimate the cost of each treatment will be no more than twenty U.S. dollars.

Curiosity, stubbornness and some measure of good sense have brought me commercial success, and they've brought me the ability to give back. I don't intend to ever stop asking how and why. I hope I never lose my sense of gratitude as well.

> *"When I can no longer create anything, I'll be done for."*
> **COCO CHANEL, FASHION DESIGNER AND PERFUMER**

# Appendix
## Resources & Checklists

**CREATIVITY, INVENTING AND BRAINSTORMING**

*Aha! 10 Ways to Free Your Creative Spirit and Find Your Great Ideas* by Jordan E. Ayan (Crown Publishing, 1997)

*Biomimicry: Innovation Inspired by Nature* by Janine M. Benyus (William Morrow & Co., 1997)

*The Complete Idiot's Guide to New Product Development* by Edwin E. Bobrow (Alpha Books, 1997) See Chapter 4, "Don't Just Sit There Waiting for Godot," for a variety of brainstorming techniques, and Chapter 5, "Where Do You Get Those Ideas From, Anyway?"

*Five Star Mind: Games and Exercises to Stimulate Your Creativity and Imagination* by Tom Wujec (Main Street Books, 1995)

*How to Think Like Leonardo Da Vinci: Seven Steps to Genius Everyday* by Michael J. Gelb (Dell Publishing, 1998)

*Ideas, Inventions and Innovations*, available from the Small Business Administration. Consult your local office, call SBA Answer Desk: 800-UASK-SBA (800-827-5722), or log on at www.sbaonline.sba.gov

*Peak Learning*, rev. ed., by Ronald Gross (Jeremy P. Tarcher, 1999)

*A Whack on the Side of the Head: How You Can Be More Creative*, by Roger Von Oech, (Warner Books, Revised Edition, 1998)

## Inventor's Reading List Addresses

*Forbes*, 800-888-9896, www.forbes.com

*Fortune*, 800-621-8000, www.fortune.com

*New York Times*, 800-NYTIMES (698-4637), www.nytimes.com

U.S. Government Printing Office, for publications such as *Survey of Current Business, Economic Report of the President, Business America: The Magazine of International Trade,* and *Official Gazette of United States Patent & Trademark Office of Commissioner of Patents and Trademarks* issued every Tuesday. Catalog available. 888-293-6498, www.gpo.gov

*U.S. News & World Report*, 800-436-6520, www.usnews.com

*Wall Street Journal*, 800-WSJ-8609, www.wsj.com (Subscription required.)

## PROTOTYPING, FUND-RAISING AND BUSINESS PLANS

### Prototyping

*SolidWorks*, designs software solutions that cover all aspects of your product development process with a seamless, integrated workflow—design, verification, sustainable design, communication and data management. www.solidworks.com

*Pro E, Pro/Engineer* is now *PTC Creo Parametric*, a full suite of 2D and 3D CAD software. www.nxrev.com

AUTOCAD *Inventor*® 3D CAD software offers an easy-to-use set of tools for 3D mechanical design, documentation, and product simulation. Digital Prototyping with *Inventor* helps you design and validate your products before they are built to deliver better products, reduce development costs, and get to market faster. Autodesk, www.autodesk.com

CADDCO, concept and CAD drawings. Call 515-547-2867, www.netins.net/showcase/caddco

California Manufacturing Technology Center, a state agency, can be reached at 800-300-CMTC for the office nearest to you, or visit the website at www.cmtc.com.

Castolite, Inc., for mold-making materials and liquid plastics. Catalog available. P.O. Box 391, Woodstock, IL 60098. 815-338-4670. www.castolite.com

Edmund Scientific Co., for a variety of parts. Catalog available. 101 E. Gloucester Pike, Barrington, NJ 08007. 800-728-6999, www.edsci.com

*Fine Scale Modeler* magazine. P.O. Box 1612, Waukesha, WI 53187. 800-533-6644. www.finescale.com

Industrial Designers Society of America, 703-759-0100. www.idsa.org

McMaster Carr Supply Co., Los Angeles, CA. A vast assortment of tools and hardware. 562-692-5911, www.mcmaster.com

United States Plastic Corp., Lima, OH. Plastic sheet, tubing, and bar stock, plus adhesives and tools for working with plastics. 800-809-4217, www.usplastic.com

## 3D Printing

*Stratasys*, can take your 3D CAD designs from on-screen to in-hand with realistic 3D models. Test form, fit and function. Print assembly tools on the fly or manufacture small quantities of production parts., www.stratasys.com

3D Systems, is a global, integrated solutions 3D printing company specializing in 3D printers, print materials, professional and consumer custom-parts services and 3D imaging and customization software. www.3dsystems.com

Makerbot, leading manufacturer of desktop 3D printers and scanners. www.makerbot.com

## Invention Developers

America Invents, invention firm of highly successful product designer Ken Tarlow. Offers full range of services, including evaluation, design, patent search, writing and drawing services. *Mind to Money* book and tapes available; 21 Golden Hind Passage, Corte Madera, CA 94925, 415-927-0311, www.americainvents.com, email: tarlowdes@aol.com

Arthur D. Little Enterprises, Inc. Contact Manager, New Business Development, 15 Acorn Park, Cambridge, MA 02140, 617-498-6685. www.adlittle.com

Battelle Development Corporation, 505 King Avenue, Columbus, OH 43201, 614-424-6424, www.battelle.org

Check the National Inventor Fraud Center, www.inventorfraud.com, for red flags to look out for.

## Financing Resources

*American Venture* magazine, a quarterly for entrepreneurs, "angel" investors, venture capitalists, and finance providers. 503-221-9981, www.avce.com

Association of Small Business Development Centers, a co-sponsorship partnership with the SBA, 703-271-8700, www.asbdc-us.org

FinanceHub.com, information and resources online for entrepreneurs and investors, www.financehub.com

*Financing the New Venture: A Complete Guide to Raising Capital from Venture Capitalists, Investment Bankers, Private Investors, and Other Sources* by Mark H. Long (Adams Media Corporation, 2000)

National Association of Small Business Investment Companies. For a list of financial institutions that deal with small independent businesses and those that work with socially or economically disadvantaged small business owners, write the Association at 666 11th Street NW, Suite 750, Washington, DC 20001. 202-628-5055, www.nasbic.org

*Pratt's Guide to Venture Capital Sources*, (Thomson Reuters), contact Venture Economics, 888-989-8373, www.ventureeconomics.com. or www.prattsguide.com

Small Business Administration. Your local Small Business Administration office can be found online, or call the SBA Answer Desk at 800-UASK-SBA (800-827-5722), www.sba.gov

Small Business Innovation Research makes early stage research and development grants. 800-382-4634, www.sbir.dsu.edu

## Crowdfunding/Crowdsourcing

Crowdfunding or Crowdsourcing funds for inventions have become extremely popular recently, and there are any number of websites that will consider your project for funding. Crowdfunding is a fairly new phenomenon. Indiegogo was the first site to launch this type of program in 2008, but many, many other sites like Kickstarter have followed in recent years.

A good source of these sorts of "people funded" sites is available at the non-profit Crowdsourcing Directory at www.crowdsourcing.org/directory

## Business Plans

*Business Plan Pro*, software by Tim Berry, Palo Alto Software. 800-229-7526, www.businessplanpro.com. *How to Write a Business Plan*, 5th ed. by Mike P. McKeever (Nolo Press, 2000)

The Small Business Administration has many business plan resources, including an online training course (www.sba.gov/classroom/bplan914.html); a self-paced, downloadable tutorial called "The Business Plan Road Map to Success (www.sba.gov/starting/businessplan.html); and the publication, "How to Write A Business Plan," by Linda Pinson and Jerry Jinnett (www.sba.gov/library/pubs/mp-32.doc)

*Your First Business Plan: A Simple Question and Answer Format Designed to Help You Write Your Own Plan*, 3rd ed., by Joseph A. Covello and Brian J. Hazelgren (Small Business Sourcebooks, 1998)

## DOCUMENTATION, DISCLOSURE AND PATENTING

### Inventor's Journals

*Inventor's Journal*, Inventions, Patents and Trademarks Co., 888-53-PATENT, www.frompatenttoprofit.com

*The Inventor's Notebook* by Fred Grissom and David Pressman (Nolo Press, 1996) 800-992-6656, www.nolo.com

### Forms

Invention Disclosure format: See Disclosure Document Program Instructions at www.uspto.gov/web/offices/pac/disdo.html for requirements and instructions.

Some forms can be downloaded from inventor-oriented websites, including www.freepatentforms.com (See pp. 174–76 for some sample forms.)

### Patenting

*Protecting Your Ideas: The Inventor's Guide to Patents* by Joy L. Bryant (Academic Press, 1998)

Trade Secret Home Page, www.execpc.com/~mhallign/

U.S. Patent and Trademark Office, www.uspto.gov, 800-786-9199 or 703-308-4357, for information, patent searches, copies of patents, complete filing and registration information, forms and advice. This should be your first stop and last word. Features Independent Inventor Resources section.

## Searches

U.S. Patent and Trademark Depository Libraries: Call for the one nearest to you, 800-PTO-9199.

U.S. Patent and Trademark Office, www.uspto.gov, search current and expired patents.

www.micropatent.com, for searches.

www.patents.ibm.com, for searches

## BASIC CONFIDENTIALITY, OR NONDISCLOSURE, AGREEMENT

### CONFIDENTIALITY AGREEMENT

_____(your name) _____ agrees to consult with

_____ (other party) _____ regarding the unique product

_____ (product name or concept) _____.

_____ (other party) _____ agrees to hold in confidence all discussions, trade secrets, recipes, client lists, purveyors, and the like learned during the course of the relationship between

_____ (your name) _____ and _____ (other party).

By signing this agreement, each signator affirms that they have the authority to make such agreements on behalf of their companies and that they shall notify all employees, contractors, assignees, agents and designees of the contents of this confidentiality agreement.

_____

Name, Date, and Company Title of other party

_____

Your Name, Date, and Title

## BASIC INVENTOR'S NOTEBOOK PAGE

Name of Invention: _____

Purpose of Invention: _____

_____

Description of Invention: _____ __

_____

_____

Sketch of Invention: _____

_____

_____

Unique Features of Invention and Their Advantages Over Existing

Technology: _____

_____

Actions Taken [discussed with so-and-so, researched materials,

made basic model, etc.]: _____

Inventor:_____ Date:_____

This confidential information is witnessed and understood by:

Witness:_____ Date:_____

Witness:_____ Date:_____

[second witness optional]

[if notebook pages are not numbered, number them yourself]

# MY BINDING ARBITRATION AGREEMENT

## ARBITRATION AGREEMENT

In the event that there is a dispute regarding any and all matters relating to our business relationship, it is agreed that the dispute shall be resolved by binding arbitration. It is further agreed that the arbitrator shall not be a lawyer and that the disputants shall not be represented by lawyers, but by themselves only.

We are fully aware of the provision of section 1282.4 of the California Code of Civil Procedure as shown below. (Or of any applicable code if this agreement is signed in any other state.)

[Sec. 1282.4 (Right to Counsel) A party to the arbitration has the right to be represented by an attorney at any proceeding or hearing in arbitration under this title. A waiver of this right may be revoked; but if a party revokes such waiver, the other party is entitled to a reasonable continuance for the purpose of procuring

an attorney. [Added Stats 1981 Ch. 460 sec. 2]

I / We hereby, with full comprehension of our rights, agree to waive our rights to be represented by an attorney at any binding arbitration and shall not ask the court to revoke such waiver.

_____

Name, Date, and Company Title of other party

_____

Your Name, Date, and Title

## PATENT ATTORNEYS

Attorneys and Agents Registered to Practice Before the U.S. Patent and Trademark Office, a PTO publication available at libraries.

Obtain attorney recommendations from an inventors association or your local Small Business Administration office.

### Manufacturing and Licensing

The Hook Appropriate Technology, helps inventors find marketers and manufacturers, 860-350-2709, www.thehooktek.com

Licensing Executives Society International, www.lesi.org

Manufacturers' Agents National Association (MANA), 877-626-2776.

www.thomasregister.com, search site for manufacturers.

### Marketing, Naming and Packaging

Demographic information, check www.demographia.com

800-USA-TRADE, connects you with a trade counselor at the Department of Commerce trained to help American exporters.

Hammacher Schlemmer Search for Invention Contest, www.hammacherschlemmer.com

*How I Made $1,000,000 in Mail Order*, rev. and updated ed. By E. Joseph Cossman (Fireside, 1993)

*Infomercial Marketing Report*, call 310-826-8810 for a sample issue of this monthly publication.

*Marketing Without Advertising* by M. Phillips and S. Rasberry (Nolo Press, 1997)

*Radical Marketing* by Sam Hill and Glenn Rifkin (Harper Business, 1999)

*Target Marketing* magazine, all about direct marketing. www.targetonline.com

*Under the Radar: Talking to Today's Cynical Consumer* by Jonathan Bond and Richard Kirshenbaum (John Wiley and Sons, 1998)

Wal-Mart Innovation Network (WIN), for inventions with zero to six-month sales histories, 417-836-5671, www.win12.com

## Packaging

*The Dieline*, www.thedieline.com is a dedicated platform for the package design industry and its practitioners, students and enthusiasts. It defines and promotes the world's best package design, and provides a place where the package design community can review, critique and stay informed of the latest trends and projects being created in the field. The Dieline has become the most visited website on package design in the world, capturing a readership spanning millions across hundreds of countries

*Package Design* magazine, www.packagedesignmag.com PO Box 1060, Skokie, IL 60076-9785 847.763.4938

*T2Design*, T2 Design & Prototype can help you create products from your invention ideas. Based in Los Angeles, California, T2 Design has successfully helped inventors with product design and development, prototypes, patent searching, market placement and manufacturing. 310-656-9922, www.t2design.com

## Trademarks

NameStormers, 512-267-1814 www.namestormers.com.

Patent and Trademark Office, see their Website for search information, or visit one of the Patent and Trademark Depository Libraries.

Thomson & Thomson, www.thomson-thomson.com, for professional trademark searches including TrademarkScan, Services & Support: 888-477-3447 http://library.dialog.com/bluesheets/html/bl0226.html.

*Trademark: How to Name Your Business and Product* by Kate McGrath and Stephen Elias (Nolo Press, 1992)

## Inventor Resources, Associations and Assistance

From Patent to Profit workshops based on the book of the same name.

A variety of other resources are available, 888-53-Patent, www.frompatenttoprofit.com

International Federation of Inventors' Associations (IFIA), www.invention-ifia.ch

National Congress of Inventor Organizations, P.O. Box 93669 Los Angeles, CA 90093, 213-878-6952, www.inventionconvention.com

United Inventors Association of the USA, P.O. Box 23447, Rochester, NY 14692, 716-359-9310, www.uiausa.org

## Websites

The Internet Invention Store, www.inventing.com, showcases inventions and new products, lists "products in need of investors, manufacturers, or licensing," and provides lists of inventor service providers.

InventNET, www.inventnet.com, The Inventor's Network.

National Inventor Fraud Center, www.inventorfraud.com, "Helping inventors through education." Includes BAD guys and GOOD guys lists.

Patent Café, www.PatentCafe.com, features Ask the Experts Message Board, Live Expert chats, and downloadable invention assessment forms.

## Newsgroups

alt.inventors, post questions and join in discussions.

misc.int.property, the legal side of patents, trademarks and copyrights.

patent-news, send subscribe, unsubscribe, help and information

requests to administrative address: Majordomo@world.std.com

## Magazines

*Entrepreneur*, 949-261-2325, www.entrepreneurmagazine.com

Inventor's Digest, 800-838-0808. www.inventorsdigest.com

## Trade Shows and Conventions

Invention Convention, 323-878-6925, www.inventionconvention.com

National Inventors' Expo, maintained by the U.S. Patent and Trademark Office. Tradeshow Central, www.tscentral.com

## BIBLIOGRAPHY

There are many resources aimed at helping inventors. To ensure that my experiences and advice might be useful and instructive, I compared notes with and sometimes cited the following:

The Baby Jogger® Website, babyjogger.com

Bobrow, Edwin E., *The Complete Idiot's Guide to New Product Development.* New York: Alpha Books, 1997.

Coca-Cola Website, www.cocacola.com

Coleman, Bob, and Deborah Neville. *The Great American Idea Book.* New York: W. W. Norton & Company, 1993.

Debelak, Don. *Entrepreneur Magazine:* "Bringing Your Product to Market." New York: John Wiley & Sons, 1997.

DeMatteis, Bob. with Mark Antonucci, *From Patent to Profit: Secrets & Strategies for Success.* Inventions, Patents & Trademarks Co., 1997.

Elias, Stephen. *Patent, Copyright & Trademark.* 2nd ed. Edited by Lisa Goldoftas. Berkeley, CA: Nolo Press, 1997.

Gelb, Michael J. *How to Think Like Leonardo Da Vinci: Seven Steps to Genius Every Day.* New York: Dell Publishing, 1998.

Gleick, James. "Patently Absurd." *New York Times Magazine,* 12 March 2000.

Goldratt, Eliyahu M. *The Goal: A Process of Ongoing Improvement.* 2nd rev. ed. Great Barrington, MA: North River Press, 1992.

Griffith, Richard, and Arthur Mayer. *The Movies.* New York: Simon and Schuster, 1970.

Hirasuna, Delphine. "Sorry, No Beige." *Apple Media Arts,* 1998, online (www. apple.com/creative/collateral/ama/ index/html)

Kawasaki, Guy, with Michele Moreno. *Rules for Revolutionaries: The Capitalist Manifesto for Creating and Marketing New Products and Services.* New York: Harper Business, 1999.

Macdonald, Anne L. *Feminine Ingenuity: Women and Invention in America.* New York: Ballantine Books, 1992.

MIT inventor's Website, www.mit.edu

"Needle Epidemic—Actions, Reactions." *San Francisco Chronicle,* 14 April 1998.

Newhouse, Elizabeth L., ed. *Inventors and Discoverers Changing Our World.* Washington, DC: National Geographic Society, 1988.

Nolo's Legal Encyclopedia, www.nolo.com

OXO Good Grips™ Website, www.oxo.com

Panati, Charles. *Panati's Extraordinary Origins of Everyday Things.* New York: Harper & Row, 1987.

Perrier Website, www.perrier.com

Pressman, David. *Patent It Yourself.* 6th ed. Berkeley, CA: Nolo Press, 1997.

Reynolds, Pat. "SKYY® Gets It Right." *Packaging World,* December 1994.

*Science Friday,* "Technology Patents." National Public Radio, 24 March 2000.

Shekerjian, Denise. *Uncommon Genius: How Great Ideas Are Born.* New York: Penguin Books, 1990.

Thomas, Robert J. *New Product Success Stories: Lessons from Leading Innovators.* New York: John Wiley & Sons, 1995.

Winship, Michael. *Television.* New York: Random House, 1988.

## ACKNOWLEDGEMENTS

My heartfelt gratitude and admiration go to Yvette Bozzini and Peter Laughlin for their intelligent, astute, and creative research and advice and for providing the perfect backup whenever one of my best stories hit a rough patch. Thanks also to Al Kolvites, Tom Hunter, and Michele Carpario for reading and commenting on parts of the manuscript; to Sam Farber and Phil Baechler for the straight scoop on their inspiring stories; and to James Connolly, Publisher at Council Oak Books, for careful editing and suggestions.

# INDEX

**RESEARCH NOTES**

**BRAINSTORMS**

## NOODLING & DOODLING

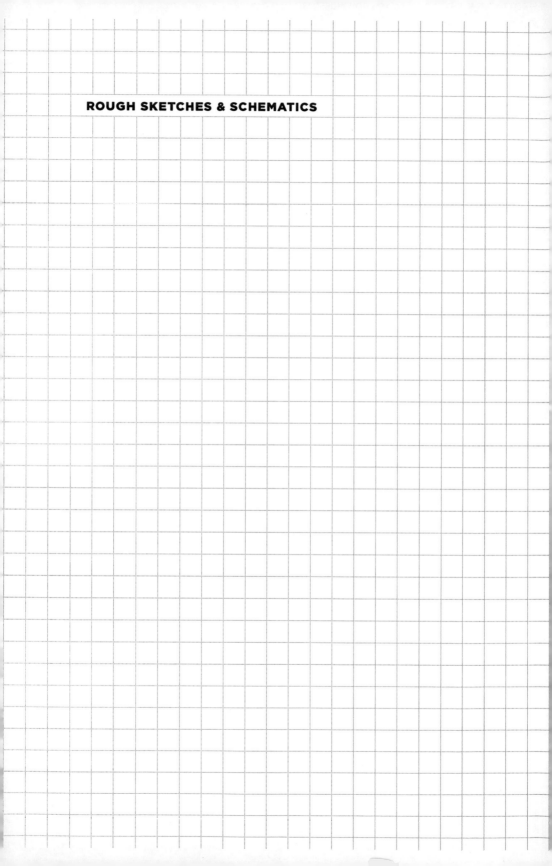

**ROUGH SKETCHES & SCHEMATICS**

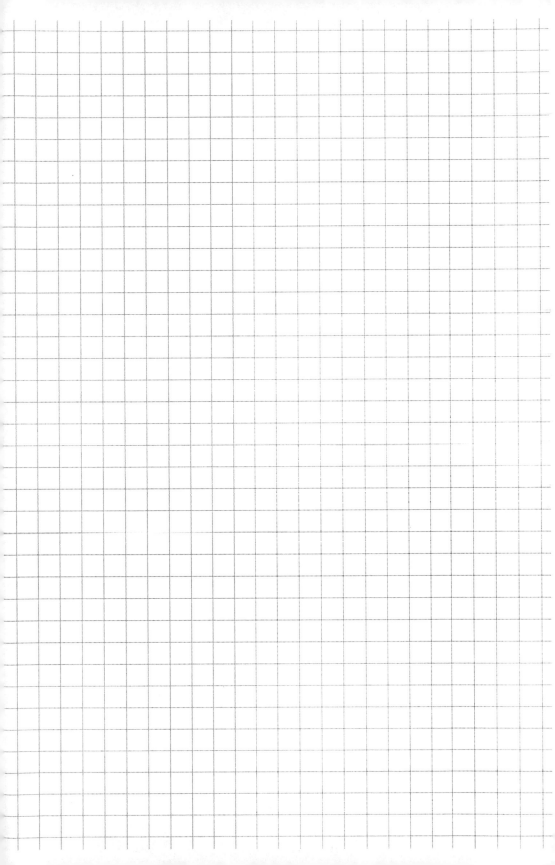

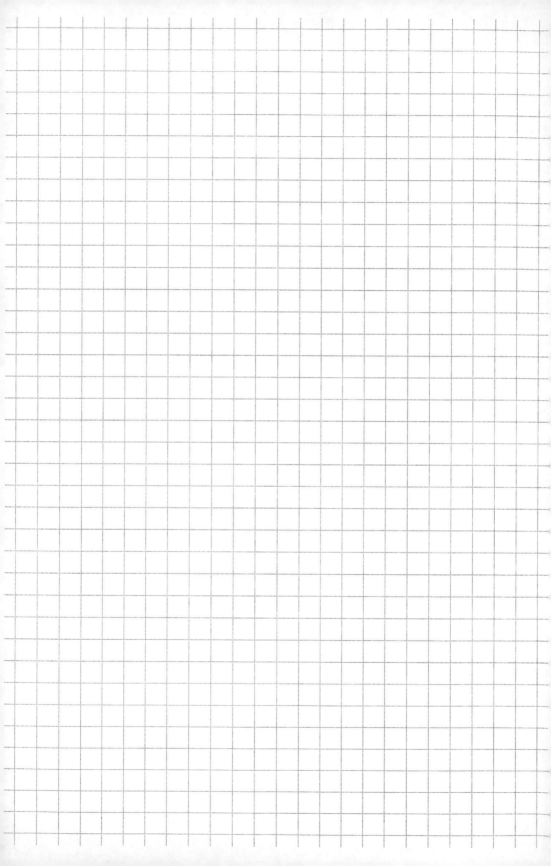

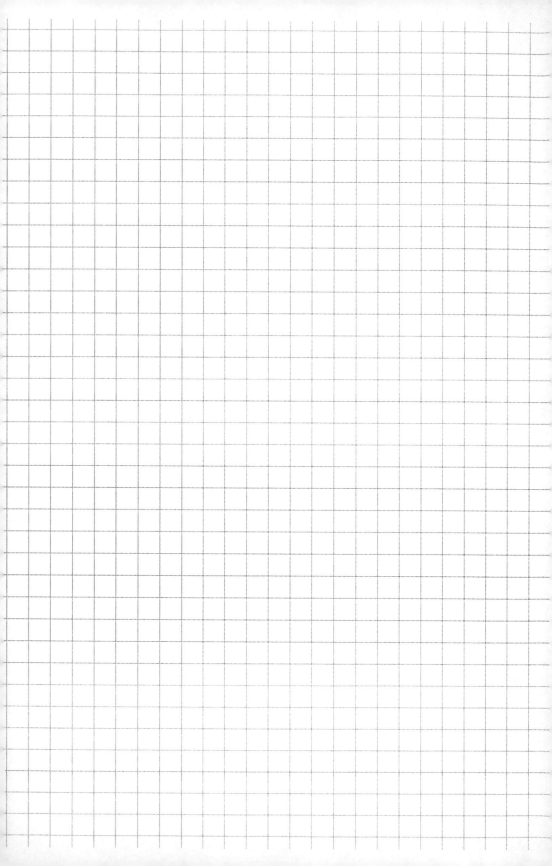

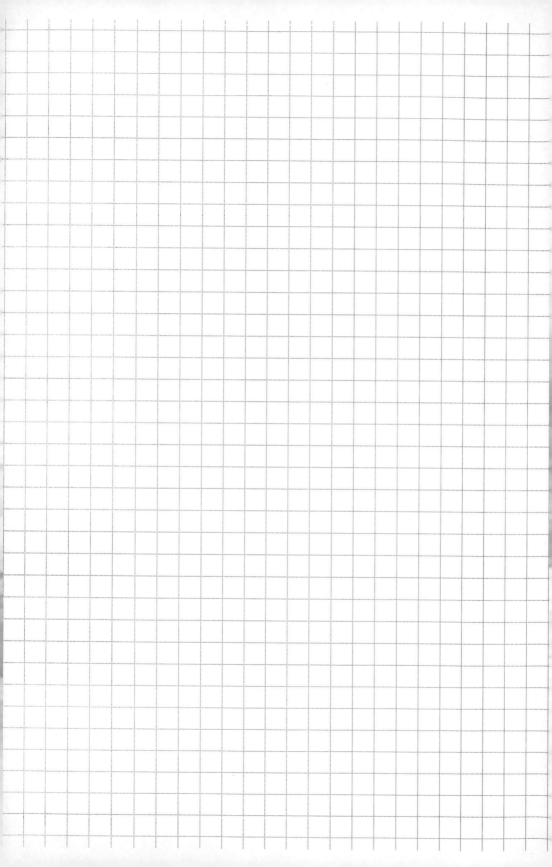

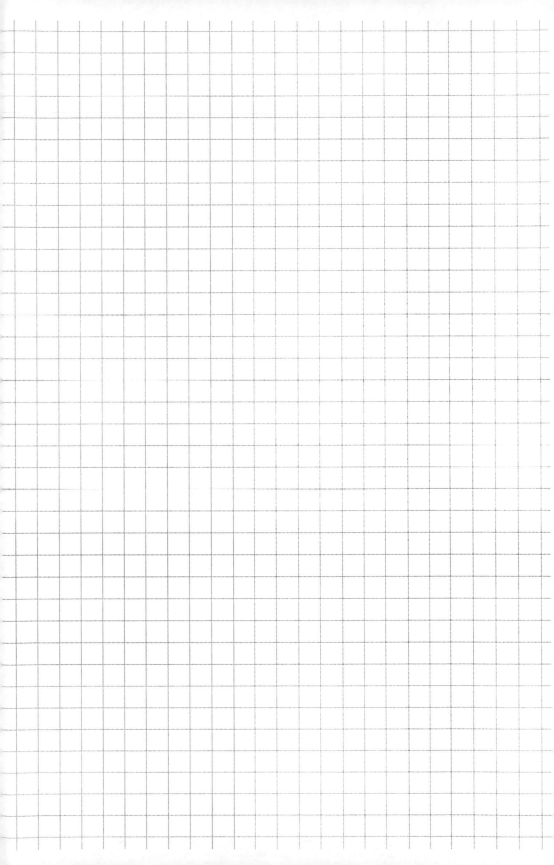

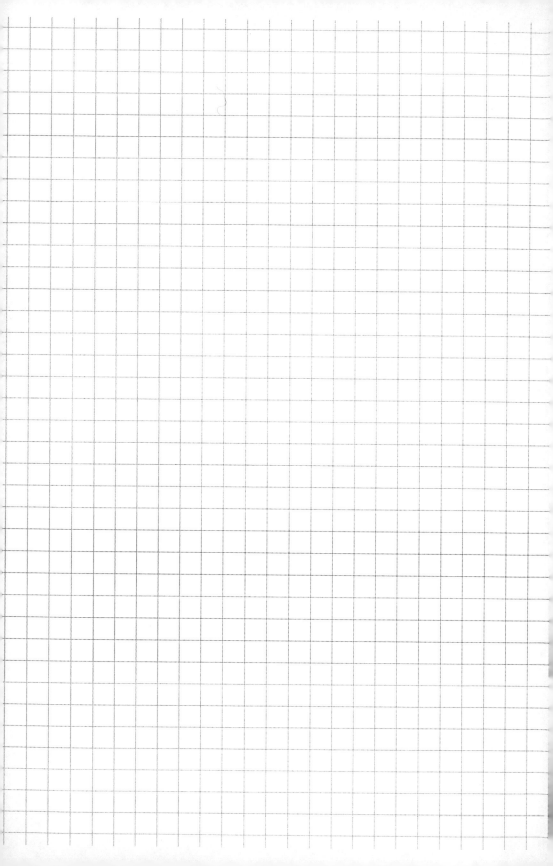

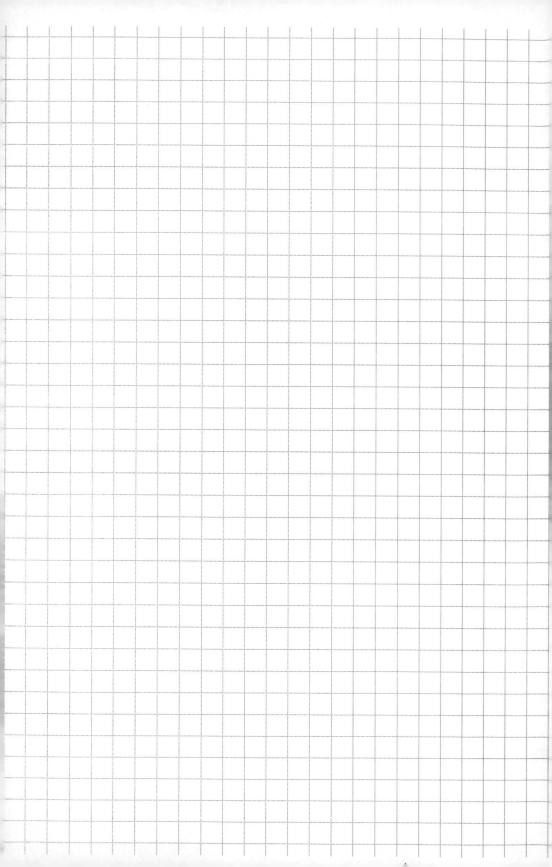

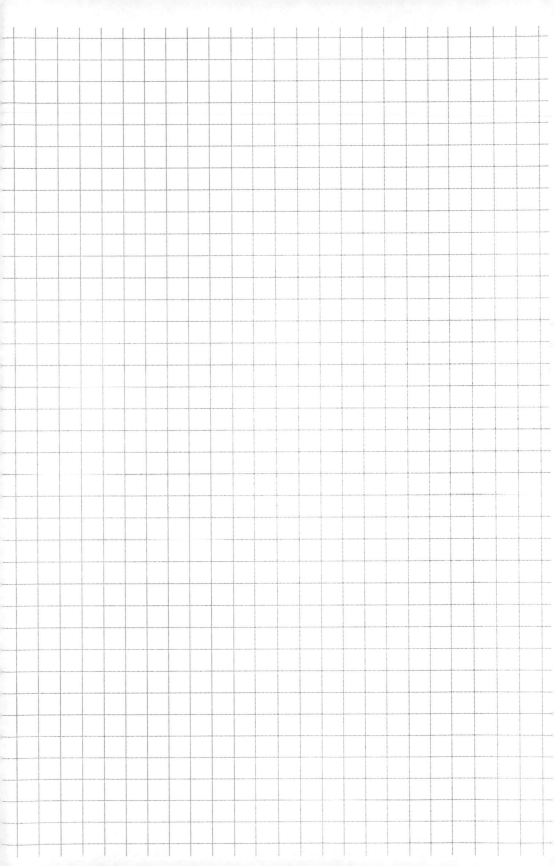

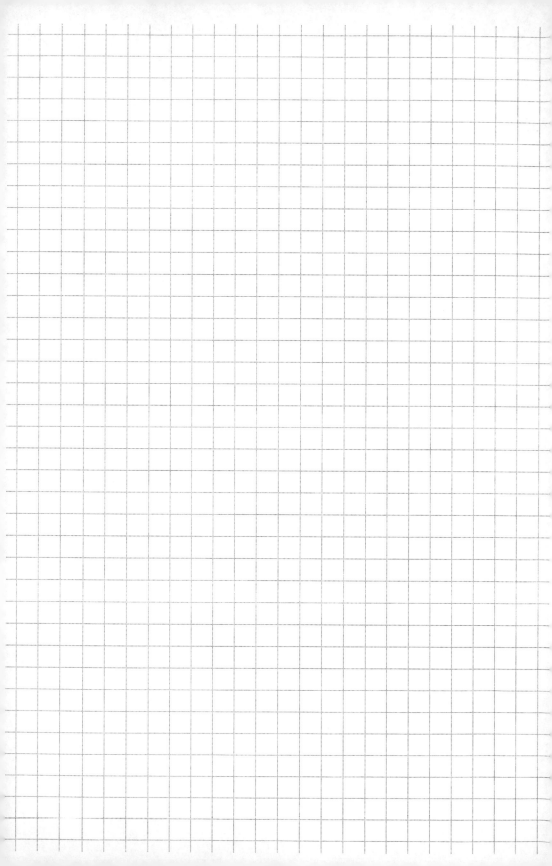

CPSIA information can be obtained at www.ICGtesting.com
Printed in the USA
LVOW07*0505051214

417283LV00004BA/6/P